The Alternative Guide To Property Investment

How To Build Your Property Portfolio Via The New Crowdfunding Platforms

Frazer Fearnhead

BlueSilver Publishing
91–95 Hale Road
Hale
Cheshire
WA15 9HW

Designed and typeset by Mach 3 Solutions Ltd (www.mach3solutions.co.uk)

ISBN 978-1-544263-25-0

Contents

About the author

I was privileged to attend one of the top academic schools in the country – Manchester Grammar School. This was followed by Leeds University and Manchester Law School.

That all led to me getting a well-paid (fairly glamorous) job as a lawyer in the music industry. But I was never quite sure how I had ended up there. In my mind, I have always been an entrepreneur.

I suppose I had no real idea what was possible at the age of 17 – there simply wasn't any 'entrepreneur' option at the careers advice centre.

Being academically successful did nothing to help me develop as an entrepreneur. In fact, I believe it hindered and delayed my progress, sending me off towards a destination where I would never be happy. Whilst education may be necessary for careers in law, banking, accountancy or medicine, I don't believe it has much to do with business success – certainly I can point to many examples of people I have known from school days who were not considered bright (or even dynamic) and didn't go to university but are now 'worth' (I hate that phrase) tens of millions … makes me sick. (Not really.)

At the age of 13, in 1982, I turned my hobby, magic, into a viable business and spent most weekends performing at children's parties, earning £50 a time. My mother still has the pictures from the local paper (and threatens to show them to people if I'm rude to her). Later, I built on my love of music and dancing, promoting my own club nights. My first event was a rather ambitious fashion show and party at the Hacienda in Manchester, which I staged at the age of 18. Over 1,000 people bought tickets and Adam, my friend/business partner, and I made over £4,000 profit in one night. I admit to feeling rather pleased with myself at the time and thinking it was so easy I would never have to worry about making money again ... that proved to be somewhat overly optimistic.

From this initial success, I went on to organise regular events at nightclubs and a number of theatre and short film productions whilst I was at university. I think the main reason these little entrepreneurial excursions were successful is that I loved what I was doing and had an intuitive sense of what would work. I should have had the confidence to stay with the activities I was passionate about but like many young people who feel pressure to 'get an education' or 'get a proper job' I took what seemed to be the sensible route.

Big mistake. But like everything, it's never too late to change. My career as a music lawyer was moderately interesting but I certainly wasn't passionate about it. The perks, though, were fantastic. It was the 1990s, Cool Britannia ruled the airwaves and there I was working in the heart of the music industry, dining with pop stars, hanging out at the Groucho and Soho House, invitations to showbiz parties, free CDs, free drinks and other things, as you can imagine.

My legal work was suffering, probably as a result of being almost permanently semi-hungover, and my relationship with my boss was becoming increasingly fractious. He was actually a great guy but we saw things quite differently. He, for example thought I should spend more time drafting documents than going to gigs and hanging out with pop stars. Though I recall he didn't complain when I brought new clients in as a result of my social activities.

Anyway, after a few months, during which I half-heartedly debated leaving, a pivotal moment occurred that made me realise I really was in the wrong job. Despite all the perks – the things, you tell yourself, that make putting up with the crap worthwhile – I knew that if I wanted to be happy I needed to be true to myself and leave.

I had just had a meeting with a new band and I told them how much I loved their music. After they left, my boss turned to me, frowned, and said, 'Frazer, "love" isn't a word lawyers use.' That one phrase decided it for me. There and then I made the decision to stop being a lawyer and that's what I did.

My friend, Adam (with whom I had hosted the Hacienda party) had just given up his job as commissioning editor of Loaded magazine and together we set up an artist/events business, BlueSilver, named after a line in a Duran Duran song.

We took shared office space in Notting Hill with ex-Radio I DJ Gary Davies who was now running his own production company and we started our first proper business. I can still remember the first Monday morning I was due to go into the office. I was absolutely petrified. It was the first and only time I have ever had a panic attack. I sat on my sofa, hyperventilating and trying to breathe in and out of a paper bag wondering if I had just made a catastrophic mistake. I mean, what kind of idiot leaves a well-paid glamorous job as a music lawyer to set up his own badly thought-out business with no definite income stream ... this kind of idiot, apparently.

No doubt if I had stayed a lawyer, I'd probably be enjoying a very large income today as partner in a top law firm – and I am often asked whether I regret leaving the law. Well, despite the financial struggles and difficulties I have faced, I can honestly say that, apart from that first morning of self-employment when all the doubts and fears rushed into my head, I have never regretted it. If such thoughts ever cross my mind I simply remind myself of how trapped I felt as a lawyer and how having the freedom to do pretty much what I want is much more valuable to me than a huge salary.

So our company did pretty well, I suppose. Surprising, as we were making it up as we went along. We created the idea of pro-celebrity five-a-side football tournaments and sold the idea to The Phoenix Festival and later the V festivals, and we subsequently organised the first national UK five-a-side football tournament in 2000 – The Millennium Cup – which was supported by *The Sun* newspaper and *Loaded* magazine.

Adam and I eventually went our separate ways, and I started to focus more on corporate events and marketing. I built the business up and, using creative branding and marketing, beat off competition from much larger more established companies to attract blue-chip clients such as BSkyB, Morgan Stanley, Granada Media, and One2One for which I arranged a variety of large-scale corporate events.

The company was starting to grow and build its reputation when 9/11 happened. On September 11th 2001 we had £600,000 worth of Christmas party bookings in the pipeline. Over the course of the next few weeks every time the phone rang it was someone calling to cancel their event, as the clients, many of them City based, did not believe it was appropriate to host a lavish party that year. A month later, we had not one Christmas party remaining. Obviously, I understand why they cancelled, but it was devastating for the company and, I guess, I lost my enthusiasm for the business after that.

So, what next?

I had been investing in property in my spare time since 1994 and after seeing an advert in the *Evening Standard* I attended a property seminar hosted by a small investment seminar business. The idea of helping other people invest in property really appealed to me and after attending the course myself and buying a couple of properties through them, I proposed to the owner that I start organising bigger events for him and help him develop his business on a success fee basis.

He agreed and I ended up working with him in a business development consultancy role for three years: creating the marketing materials, organising seminars, developing a franchisee programme and recruiting franchisees. We did very well and I learned a great deal from this role and, not to put too fine a point on it, I thought I could do a better job myself. So in 2005, I launched my own web-based property investment consultancy: The Armchair Property Investor.

I started with literally nothing. The first client was someone I already knew and with the money earned from that deal I got the logo designed and a website built. It was definitely a case of the right place/right time for the business – property investment had become something of a national pastime and in the first six months alone Armchair promoted and sold over £11 million worth of new-build property.

Thanks to the innovative concept, the branding, and clever marketing the company won the award for Best Start Up Business 2006 (North West Development Agency/*Entrepreneur* magazine) and I was subsequently approached by two larger companies interested in purchasing the company. I initially rejected their offers but a year later, my gut instinct told me that the business was becoming more and more difficult (primarily because mortgage deals had dried up) and it might need the support of a larger organisation if the company was to survive. I subsequently sold Armchair in 2007 (just two years after its incorporation) for £2.25 million. Given what happened to the property market six months later, it was the best thing I could have done, but if I am honest, I cannot say to what extent the decision was pure luck and how much was instinctive business acumen. Possibly, a little of both.

Following the sale of Armchair, I left the property market for a few years and spent my time as a consultant helping business owners market their business more effectively. Around 2010, I realised the property market was beginning to pick up and there were great opportunities in acquiring repossessed properties at bargain prices. I was approached by some old clients and began sourcing deals for them as well. The trouble was, mortgages were virtually impossible to obtain so it was only the very cash-rich investors who were able to capitalise on the market. It was very frustrating.

Inspired by the likes of crowdfunding platforms, Kickstarter and Crowdcube, I came up with the idea to cut out the banks and join like-minded people together to invest in property for mutual profit. At the time, property crowdfunding simply didn't exist anywhere in the world and I was told by a succession of lawyers that such a business was prohibited by the Financial Services and Markets Act. I persevered. I researched that Act, found exceptions to the rules and eventually, after six months searching, managed to find solicitors that agreed we could operate legally, provided we worked within very strict parameters of the exceptions set out in the Act.

And so, in March 2012, I launched what was the world's first property crowdfunding platform – The House Crowd – and gave birth to a rapidly growing industry that is now worth billions.

Five years on, The House Crowd has raised over £40 million from our database of 15,000 'crowdfunding' investors – investing as little as £1,000 each – and has evolved from purchasing £50,000 terraced houses, to financing multi-million-pound new-build developments.

I strongly believe that property remains, despite the government's recent attacks on landlords, the best way to invest for your future and that, for most people, doing so through crowdfunding is the best (and perhaps the only) way to make property part of their investment portfolio.

This books explains why.

Introduction

Alternative finance platforms (both equity and peer-to-peer (P2P)) have grown exponentially since The House Crowd kick-started the industry in 2012. Within the alternative finance space, real estate crowdfunding is by far the largest and most popular sector.

In 2015 alone, the UK property crowdfunding industry generated £700M worth of investment. Investment at present comes from a mix of 'early adopters', internet savvy private investors and institutional money. But as the general population becomes more aware of the possibilities of property crowdfunding, the global real estate crowdfunding industry is forecast to grow to $250B by 2020.

Property crowdfunding offers both highly attractive returns (especially given poor interest rates on savings and pitiful annuity rates) and, unlike with stock market investments, it can provide reasonably predictable and consistent returns backed by the security of being UK property.

A recent survey of over-55s showed that a 'lost generation' of those nearing the end of their working lives are facing a bleak retirement:

- 41% say their hopes for a financially secure retirement are no longer possible.
- Over a third (37%) say their lifestyle will be worse once they retire with just 16% believing it will improve.
- Over a quarter (26%) say it's too late to change their plans and save more for their retirement.

The survey revealed that over-55s know that their plans for retirement are inadequate, yet feel they are powerless to change their fate:

- One in five (20%) blame the government for not being able to save for retirement.
- On average, those surveyed said they'd like their annual income to be £18,235 once retired – but think in reality they will only receive £14,180.
- 51% do not have a personal pension, and do not plan to put one in place.
- Over a quarter (28%) do not have a workplace pension, and do not plan to put one in place.
- This indicates a significant number of today's over-55s are planning to rely on their state pension.

Women feel even less positive about their retirement than men: just 17% of women said they are prepared financially for retirement, while 28% of men reported being on track. Women were also more likely to blame the government for being unable to save for their retirement (23%, versus 18% of male respondents).

As of 2017, a very large majority of the population are not aware of property crowdfunding or, if they have heard of it, do not understand how it works or how it can benefit them.

Financial advisers are expensive and, in any event, even if they understand the concept (which many do not) are unlikely to recommend any product that is not fully regulated as it will not be covered by their professional indemnity insurance.

In short, there is a serious problem which is going to lead to general suffering as people reach retirement age. I believe property crowdfunding, whilst it may not entirely solve the problem, could certainly help alleviate it for those who participate.

The purpose of this book therefore is to set out in layman's terms:

- why property makes for an attractive investment (but feel free to skip this section if you already know why);
- why it should be part of everyone's investment portfolio;
- how to determine your own investment criteria;
- how to invest passively in property;
- how to make it part of your portfolio even if you don't have large amounts of money to invest;

- a detailed explanation of how property crowdfunding/peer-to-peer lending works;
- the risks;
- how the process works;
- how to decide whether it is right for you;
- how to choose a suitable platform(s) to invest in.

Chapter 1

Why invest in property at all?

Fact: almost everybody wants to be able to retire at some point and enjoy the later years of their lives in comfort.

If you think the state pension will allow you to do that, then, sorry, you are living in La La Land. The government will not look after you in your later years. It simply can't afford to.

The maximum state pension in 2016/17 is £119.30 per week. Can you live comfortably on that? In fact, can you live on that at all?

It is imperative that you do something to supplement that. Your main choices are:

- savings accounts
- a private pension
- shares
- property

I will dealing with each of these briefly.

Savings accounts

We are always being told that keeping your money in a bank account is safe and it's guaranteed – at least up to £75,000. That is provided the government doesn't also go bankrupt, which is not as ridiculous as it might sound; it would have happened here in the 1970s had the IMF not stepped in, and just take a look at Greece and Italy and Portugal and Spain ... oh yes, and France, to see how vulnerable many governments are right now. I do not believe saving your money in a bank account is in any way a sensible manner to provide for your retirement. The only thing that is guaranteed is that the value of that money is being eroded year on year by inflation, and given the current rates of interest payable the net value is actually decreasing. Even if you had a million pounds saved by the time you retired at, say, 2% interest, that would only provide you with £20,000 a year income – and that's before tax.

Pensions

So, let's look at private pensions ... The days of the final salary pension are long gone, and few, if any, private pensions have delivered what clients expected while some, it's fair to say, have been outright disasters. The returns, whilst clearly considerably better than a savings account, are still negligible and the only people, in my opinion, who seem to really profit are the institutions that provide them.

We've seen pension fund after pension fund collapse, leaving thousands with substantial losses, executives ripping off their firms and employees for millions, and major holes appearing in the entire 'safety-net' structure. Robert Maxwell and the Mirror Group and British Home Stores are just two of a number of pension funds that spring to mind.

Please read Chapter 3 if you need convincing that the pension most people have is nowhere near enough to generate an annuity that will finance a comfortable retirement.

So whilst you definitely do need a vehicle to provide for your retirement, it definitely does not need to be an institutional or company pension.

Investing in shares

Clearly fortunes can be made in the stock market – if you know what you are doing. If you don't, then picking the best tracker fund you can find would seem the most sensible option. I would not advocate against investing in the stock market but in my opinion it is considerably more volatile than property and there are many more factors beyond your control that make it harder to invest in successfully.

Property

Of all the investment options available, I believe property is the one people most easily understand and, therefore, are most likely to be successful with. I mean, let's face it, even Goldman Sachs didn't really understand what they were peddling in the noughties. The more complicated something is, the more likely it is that investors don't really know what they are doing or what the risks are. They don't even know what it is they don't know, so how can they possibly evaluate the risks? The only way forward is to rely on 'reputable' institutions to advise them … and we all know where that path leads. Do I really need to recap all the scandals caused by supposedly reputable and regulated financial institutions over the last 20 years and how many billions of people's money have been misappropriated or wasted: endowments; Enron; Lloyds; PPI; securitisation of subprime mortgages and giving them AAA ratings; Axa, Goldman Sachs and others selling their clients what they knew to be worthless investments; interest rate default swaps; fixing LIBOR rates, etc., etc.

It is clear that the size of an organisation does not denote integrity and that regulatory bodies do little but shut the door after the horse has bolted and punish the stable boys … but rarely the owners.

I believe in trusting your own judgement and managing your own money. If you don't know how, then learn, otherwise you will always be at the mercy of someone else's honesty.

Property allows you to do that. Bricks and mortar are real, not smoke-and-mirror financial products. And just about everyone with an average IQ can grasp the basic finances and see how income or profit is likely to be made. Whether it is made or not is a different matter, but you can put the odds in your favour – if you educate yourself.

It is also an asset class that allows you to use leverage which can multiply your profits, can produce instant gains if you buy from a someone motivated to sell quickly, provide steady income and historically has increased in value on average at around 7% a year.

It's not hard to see why it appeals to so many people.

But until 2012, property investment was limited to individuals with readily available capital and a credit rating sufficient to acquire mortgages. And, after 2007, it became increasingly difficult for even those individuals to obtain mortgages; the banks, being ultra-conservative, would turn down applications or change their mind at the last minute for all sorts of spurious reasons.

One of the downsides of property that puts many people off is that it is usually not a passive investment. The process of finding, purchasing and applying for a mortgage is time consuming, and managing properties, tenants, and the maintenance requirements, not to mention the red tape, can be burdensome.

The arrival of property crowdfunding changed all that. As we will see in the following chapters, the reasons for the success of the alternative finance industry in real estate are numerous. The benefits to lenders and investors, as well as developers, buyers and tenants themselves, have helped make the disruptive force of property crowdfunding such a popular vehicle for investment. It has democratised property investment allowing virtually everybody to invest, and start to build a healthily diversified portfolio.

The industry represents a new era for how we invest, how we manage the increasing demand for property in the UK, and – crucially – how we create a continually stable, profitable economy for ourselves, and for the next generation.

As with shares, property has the ability to provide you with both capital growth and passive income that grows steadily over time as rents increase – an income stream that continues well into your retirement, to supplement any annuity from a pension pot.

However, I believe property investment has several potential major advantages over investing in shares. This is how people have managed to make fortunes from property – though as you will read later, it is now a lot harder to do so.

1.   You can borrow to buy

Imagine asking your bank manager to lend you £100,000 so you can go and buy stocks and shares, or commodity futures. He'd tell you to stop wasting his time! But that same manager may very well be happy to lend you £100,000 to buy a house. Why is that?

Well, the most important factor for the bank is that, if you default on your loan, the bank can take possession of a solid asset that can then be sold on. And, based on historical performance, there's a low level of risk that, in the event of a default, the bank will be left with an asset worth less than the money owed on it – well, unless of course, they start granting 125% LTV (loan to value) mortgages, in which case it's likely to be a different story ... as we all know.

From your point of view, this offers a wonderful opportunity: for, for, example, £20,000 you could obtain an 80% LTV mortgage and take ownership of an appreciating asset worth £100,000. If it appreciates by 10% in the first year, which is not uncommon, especially if you have bought wisely – you will have made £10,000.

That's 50% return on capital employed (ROCE) in 12 months. Now it's entirely possible to make similar or greater gains with shares in a particular company, but for every high-returning stock there are usually a number of losers. With property, it's much easier to pick winners most of the time.

This ability to borrow relatively easily makes property much more powerful than any other traditional asset class.

And of course, if structured correctly, the rent you receive should cover the cost of financing, and the cost of managing and maintaining the property.

2. Market value

It is the very nature of the stock market that you are always buying at the current market value market value (which can change massively from day to day (or even hour to hour). As we know with property, it is possible to find or negotiate deals so you can buy property at less than market value and make instant margins – sometimes as high as 25% or 30%.

3. Refinance

You can refinance property from time to time at very low rates and do not need to sell your assets to take out large sums. You can do so without paying any tax on the money you withdraw (at that point – after all, it's just a secured loan) and keep your assets working for you.

4.   Property is an illiquid asset

That has both advantages and disadvantages and means it is not attractive for those who like more volatile investments where fortunes can be made (or lost) quickly. But I am not a gambler nor do I wish to become an expert in share trading, which takes a huge amount of education and experience – I like the stability of property. There is no need for constant monitoring. You could easily take your eye off the market for months without any fear that your assets have plummeted in value.

5.   Control

As mentioned above, I believe in looking after your own destiny and managing your own finances. What I like about property is that I can use my own initiative and knowledge to improve a property and increase its value. By contrast, with the stock market, the company directors hold all the decision-making power including the power to distribute profit as they see fit. I am confident of my own abilities and prefer to rely on my judgement rather than that of others I don't even know, so this is a major advantage of property investment for me.

6.   Macroeconomic factors

In addition to the five factors above there are certain macroeconomic factors specific to the UK that make property investment in this country a particularly sound proposition. It is, to a very large extent, a simple economic law of supply and demand that will continue to exert upward pressure on house prices and will not change, however much the government tries to interfere, with the housing market.

Put simply, that means if the demand for something is greater than the supply, then the price for that thing will inevitably rise.

This law of supply and demand works particularly strongly for the residential market. At any one time, all individuals in the UK (with few exceptions) are living in either owned or rented property. As such, if there is a shortage of supply, then there must be upward pressure on either rental or purchase values.

We live on a small island, and the population is growing by around 400,000 people a year.

The number of people living in the UK is forecast to rise from 64.6 million in 2014 to 74.3 million by 2039, according to the Office for National Statistics.

Not only that, but within the population, the demand for more housing is continually increasing, because there are more single people (unmarried, living alone): a 30% increase in the last 10 years. There is a rising divorce rate (necessitating two homes), there are more students in further education (student accommodation), people are living longer (retirement property), immigration continues to increase despite resistance to it from certain sectors of society, and the average household size is shrinking.

All this means the demand for housing is getting greater and greater. The supply simply cannot keep up. It is conservatively estimated that the UK requires at least 200,000 new homes a year. In 2015, 142,890 new homes were built. That's a shortfall of 57,110 in just one year. And that shortfall is getting larger each and every year.

Due to land use restrictions, a seemingly all-prevailing NIMBYism hampering new developments, the fact that most councils are massively obstructive when it comes to developers acquiring planning permission plus an increasing shortage of skilled craftsmen, the house building industry has zero chance of keeping up with demand; and every year there is a large shortfall which means the imbalance is getting worse. By 2020 it is estimated there will be a shortfall of around 500,000 properties. It doesn't take an economist to work out what that will do to house prices.

So, despite any temporary dips in demand or oversupply, it is apparent that long-term demand is set to outstrip supply and this will inevitably lead to house price growth. This will apply particularly to one- and two-bed properties as the average household is shrinking in size.

But is this sustainable – what if the market crashes?

The press publish articles (many of them contradictory) on an almost daily basis about what the property market is doing. There is always a lot of chatter about house prices crashing. Well, it has happened before – look back over the last 30 years and you will see the same stories again and again (most recently 2008, before that 1990 and, before that, during the Oil Shock of 1972) and it may well happen again.

However, if you are investing sensibly and either investing in short-term deals with a defined exit or holding out for the long term, I do not believe you need to fear a property crash, as the graph below illustrates.

The average house price in the UK in September 2016 was £217,888. This has increased from £172,972 in 2010, and from £202,389 in 2015. In the north-west alone, the most increasingly prosperous market outside London, average house prices rose nearly 6% within the period September 2015–16.

Average house prices	
1960	£2,530
1970	£4,975
1980	£23,596
1990	£59,785
2000	£101,550
2006	£160,000
2010	£172,972
2016	£217,888

Source ODPM

If, for example, using the graph above, you had put down a 10% deposit on an average house in 2006 (which was the worst possible time as it was when prices were close to their peak), and then were forced to sell between 2008 and 2010, you would probably have incurred a loss as property prices fell. But if you had held on until 2010 you probably would have got your money back and if you had waited and sold in 2016 you would have made a profit of around £50,000 on your initial £16,000 investment. Maybe not what you would have liked over 10 years, but hardly a disaster either.

You need to be sure you never become a 'motivated seller'. If you're thinking about setting up a property portfolio for the short term, there's a chance you'll be caught in, and hurt by, any price correction. But if you're in it for the long haul, and you have things set up correctly and with the right balances in place, then short-term corrections shouldn't present a major problem. Even major events like Brexit seem to have a very short-term effect. Therefore, always make sure you can cover your costs and can keep the property rented until conditions favour a sale.

Of course, those are just 'average' house prices and as you will read later on, with property it's relatively easy to beat those averages by selecting investments more carefully.

Real estate investments potentially offer both capital gains and regular income. Purchased at the right price, instant profits are also possible. Changes in use, gaining planning permission and simple refurbishments can all instantly increase value. They also have a low correlation with traditional asset classes like stocks and bonds. As such, it is an excellent asset class to have as part of your portfolio.

And whilst traditional wisdom suggests that a well-constructed investment portfolio should contain a healthy mix of assets, I am not convinced. I prefer to stick with what I know – property – and diversify within that one asset class. But even though you may well disagree with me (and I am sure most people will), I think I have made a strong case for why property should be part of every investment portfolio, however widely diversified.

Chapter summary

- You need to provide for the later years of your life.
- You must not rely on the government to do that.
- Historically, property has proven to be the best investment.
- Investing in property was previously only accessible if you had a substantial deposit and good credit rating.
- Crowdfunding has democratised property investment, opening it up to the general population.

Chapter 2

How much diversification is sensible?

In the previous chapter I mentioned that I go against traditional wisdom as I am not particularly convinced about diversification across different asset classes as one cannot possibly be knowledgeable about all of them and therefore must seek to rely on third-party advisers. If you have no time or inclination to look after your own money this is probably sage advice. I accept that for most people there are good reasons to do so but, for me, I would point to the fact that one of the wealthiest people I have ever met invests all his money in property. But not just in any property, and not just in one particular area, but in one particular street (in central London). He won't even consider buying properties on adjoining streets. As far as he is concerned, they are outside his area of expertise. Clearly, specialisation can have its advantages.

Therefore, I am not giving advice, just telling you what I personally think. The consensus of opinion about diversification may be generally sensible for most people but may not be right for everyone, especially for those who are experts in their field. That's a matter for you to decide.

What I do think is sensible for most people is to diversify and spread your risk (within reason) so all your eggs are not in in one basket. And one reason I believe property crowdfunding is such a beneficial concept is that it allows you to spread whatever available capital you have over a number of different properties so, if a disaster befalls one, you don't have all your money tied up in it and you still have others to fall back on.

Within the asset class 'property' itself, you could if you wish diversify your portfolio in a number of different ways. It could include traditional buy-to-let properties, new-build apartments, commercial investments, HMOs (houses in multiple occupation) and 'fixer-uppers'. Secured lending and development finance are other options that fall within the property investment umbrella, as you lend out sums to property developers and business owners who own property they can use as security.

Diversification also means a selection of risk profiles. Of course, you should take into account your personal circumstances and lifestyle requirements, as well as your own attitude to risk. Typically, higher risk investments come with the prospect of higher rewards, whilst a safer investment may yield lesser gains.

Buy-to-let has been the most popular option for property investment. Private renting has almost doubled in the period from 2003 to 2015, and in Manchester it has almost quadrupled, from 6% to 20%. This means in theory the buy-to-let sector should offer great potential for investment over the coming years. However, as we shall learn later, the traditional way of purchasing single buy-to-let properties may no longer be the best way to capitalise upon this growing market. In fact, it may not be feasible at all for most individuals any more.

The commercial property market, too, can be a good option. Investing in commercial real estate can mean:

- positive leverage (potentially increasing ROI (return on investment);
- tax benefits (proper structuring can offer an array of benefits tied to interest, depreciation and so on);
- more control (personal ownership equals control);
- a hedge against inflation (such property tends to benefit long term from inflation);
- cash flow and current income (rental income from stable commercial real estate means a potentially steady and predictable income stream);
- historically strong returns (average annual return: 9.5% sustained over a 20-year period).

You can find out more about commercial property and how it compares with residential property investment later in this book.

Chapter summary

- Most agree that it is sensible to have a diverse investment portfolio.
- However, question the traditional wisdom – how true is that for you?
- The greater the diversification the less expert you can become and the more reliant you are on third parties for advice.

Chapter 3

Why property investing is the best vehicle to supplement your pension

Research from Saga Investment Services (amongst various others that reached the same conclusions) has found that the UK's over-50s population needs to double the amount of pension contributions they are making, if they are to stand any chance of a decent income through their retirement.

The research found that the majority of those over-50s surveyed believed they'd need an average annual income of £15,200 to get them through their retirement (personally I cannot imagine trying to subsist on such an amount in my old age – especially given inflationary factors). The people surveyed estimated that they could generate this from a pension pot of £143,830 on average. Their estimated figures fall shockingly short of reality.

A pension pot of this size would actually generate just £7,940 guaranteed income a year (for a healthy 65-year-old) for life. That's nearly a 50% shortfall. Basically, they need double the size of their pension just to make ends meet.

To have a comfortable life, which respondents identified as being defined by holidays, dining out, socialising, and hobbies, it was calculated that they'd need at least £21,630 (clearly they are less profligate than me). That would require a pension pot of nearly £400,000 – double the respondents' estimate of £194,000 (which would generate just £10,170 guaranteed income a year).

On their estimated required sum, their pension fund would be exhausted within 12 years.

Poor returns, excessive fees and inconsistent annuity rates: a pension sure ain't what it used to be. It's no surprise, then, that people are starting to look for alternative ways of generating money for their retirement.

Research suggests that property investment is turning out to be twice as popular as any other form of investment with the over-50s. The younger generation, too, are turning down traditional pension plans, focusing instead on property investments (and now crowd-funding as a means to access the asset class). As mentioned previously, the number of people choosing – or being forced – to rent, due to the difficulty of getting into the property market, or simply because it's more convenient in many ways, is rising rapidly.

A pension also has the disadvantages of limited (and badly publi-cised) choice of annuity provider and the fact the money is inaccessible.

When it comes to cashing in, holders are often disappointed to find that they are unable to access their lump sum when they wish to without severe financial penalties. And despite recent changes, one can only access 25% of one's pension pot without incurring punitive taxation.

Not only that, as far as I know, the benefits of a pension end when the holder dies. That means you could have saved £400,000 in your pension, purchased an annuity with that, at age 65, and receive £21,000 a year thereafter. But if you were to pass away within a few years your spouse and heirs would receive nothing. The pension company keeps everything. Clearly, this is not the case if you buy a property, which can be inherited; though the Treasury will, no doubt, steal as much of it as they can. Did I say 'steal' – how outrageous, that I should accuse our esteemed government of 'stealing' money that has already had tax paid on it at least once before – in the form of income tax, stamp duty, tax on savings interest, dividend tax, etc. I do apologise. Clearly, it's perfectly fair for them to take whatever they feel like.

Whilst it is important to start saving for retirement as early in life as possible, the younger generations are waiting later and later before considering their retirement planning. This may be in part due to high living costs and stagnating real earnings amongst the young ... or, perhaps, their preference for electronic gadgets, dining out, designer clothes and foreign holidays over prudent saving ... Just saying!

This means that there is considerable concern around how this generation are going to fund their later years. I believe those who invest sensibly in property from a young age can realistically expect a much larger retirement fund than if they were to put their money in a pension even after taking into consideration the tax breaks afforded to pension contributions. For those who may have left it until their 40s or 50s, before considering their retirement income, investing in property may be their only way to catch up and generate a decent retirement income – it is simply not possible for most people to make high enough pension contributions in 15–25 years to purchase a decent-sized annuity. That's an absolute fact.

As far as property goes, rental yields are increasing and landlords are seeing better returns than they have for a long time. Manchester is currently at the top of the leader board in terms of rental yield (and potential for capital growth). Rental yields in the northern city are pushing 7% (as of July 2016): higher than any other major UK location.

There are, however, problems with buy-to-let investing. The main drawback is that it's normally very time consuming and if you don't know what you are doing and get it wrong your mistakes can cost you an awful lot of money. That's why the regulatory authorities keep telling you how risky it is ... because they think people are essentially stupid and can't make decisions for themselves.

I don't agree with them. As adults, you should be perfectly capable of making your own decisions and should be allowed to do so, unfettered by pinstriped bureaucrats who think they know better than you. But I also recognise that people don't seem very willing to accept the consequences of those decisions and take responsibility for their own judgement, if they turn out badly, so ... maybe, those pinstriped bureaucrats do have a point after all.

With property, you need to spend a considerable time researching, carrying out due diligence, comparing similar properties/sale prices, negotiating deals, arranging finance, etc. Maintenance of the property, managing tenants, and so on, also take time and money.

Older investors, in particular, are less willing to engage with the jobs involved in letting out properties, and are among the majority of those who view the relative passivity of crowdfunding as a benefit to this form of investment.

In addition to the normal headaches associated with buy-to-let, the government, in the last couple of years, has launched what many regard to be an outright war on landlords and it could be persuasively argued that buy-to-let investing, at least in the form in which it has been thriving for the last 20 years is, if not quite dead, then severely wounded. More on this later in the book.

Chapter summary

- The majority of people have not made anywhere near adequate provisions to enable them to stop working at any point.
- Regulators impose their values and opinions on everyone but are often wrong.
- Answer the question of whether you believe a pension is better than property investment given your own circumstances

Chapter 4

Establishing your own investment criteria

We held a dinner for our top-20 investors recently and I think it's fair to say that just about everybody had different reasons for investing and slightly different criteria for choosing what to invest in.

Before investing any money, you need to consider what you want to achieve. Do you want to sit back and let your investment grow in value (e.g. stamps or wine or a pension fund, if you still think that's a good idea) or do you want to generate an income (e.g. shares or property)?

Or perhaps a mix of the two?

Do you solely want to provide for your retirement and reinvest any income generated or do you need to earn an immediate income from your investments?

Are you prepared to risk all your capital on the same sort of investment or do you want to make some ultra-safe investments and speculate with a certain portion of your money on riskier but potentially more lucrative investments?

These are just a few of the questions you should ask yourself as the answers will help formulate your own investment criteria. If you have decided that you want to invest some of your capital into property, then the two most significant decisions you need to make are whether you want the emphasis to be on capital growth or cash flow and whether you want to make commercial or residential property investments.

Chapter 5

Capital growth v cash flow

Capital growth is a very powerful concept. As Albert Einstein once said, compound capital growth is the eighth wonder of the world. What compound growth means is that if an asset worth £100,000 increases in value by 10% a year it will only take eight years for that asset to be worth more than double its original value. In ten years it will be worth around £259,000. And that's without leverage.

Imagine that you're back in 1996. You have £16,000 to invest, but you're not sure what to do with it. Your stockbroker tells you one thing, your financial adviser tells you another, and your bank manager – of course – reckons you should stick it in the bank for a rainy day. Instead, you decide to use that £16,000 as a deposit on an £80,000 buy-to-let property in London (that was the average house price in London just 20 years ago).

Two decades on, the average London property is worth over £488,000. That means, provided you covered your mortgage payments and costs with rental income, your £16,000 has turned into £408,000 profit. Now there may well have been various incidental costs to take into account but, I think it's fair to say, you would still have done many times better than if you had put that money into a pension or kept it in the bank.

It's not possible to make the benefits of property investment any clearer than that. It is, in my opinion, far and away the best investment you can make. Imagine that property only did half as well as this over the next ten years. It would still be likely to produce several times the returns of any other asset class.

Because of the power of compound growth, many people think property is all about capital growth, and that aspect is certainly what helps make it an attractive investment. And the fact that you can leverage purchases and obtain, for example, an 80% LTV mortgage multiplies the rate at which your capital can grow at astonishing rates.

However, many people have come unstuck by leveraging highly and speculating on capital growth. They have then found themselves in an unsustainable position having to subsidise mortgage payments as the rental income has not been sufficient to cover their financial outgoings on the property. You may be able to support one property at £200 a month whilst you wait for it to increase in value, but how many more of those could you afford? However, if all your properties at least 'wash their face' and produce a small profit from rental income, you can support as many of them as you can buy – and benefit from the capital growth in all of them.

When choosing investments, therefore, it is never wise to over-stretch yourself and make yourself vulnerable to the banks. You must ensure that (allowing for possible interest rate rises) you have enough rental income to at least cover your borrowing, insurance, and maintenance costs as well as making an allowance for void periods and for keeping a contingency fund for repairs.

Provided that box is checked, your selection of property will depend on how important cash flow is as opposed to capital growth. Now, although historically, as I have stated, property has increased in value, on average, at around 7% a year (Office of National Statistics), more popular areas tend to increase faster than other areas (supply and demand) and larger houses tend to increase more than apartments (in general).

There is no guarantee that prices will rise consistently or will do so in respect of the particular property you have chosen. To invest purely on the basis of capital growth is a bit like gambling – though if you educate yourself well and choose your property carefully you can do very well from it.

On the whole, however attractive capital growth may sound, it is speculative and property prices, as we all know, can go up as well as down, especially in the short term. In our opinion, investing in cash-generating properties that put money in your pocket each year should be the bedrock of an investment strategy. If they are profitable, then it is easier to choose when to sell them and do so at an advantageous time.

Chapter 6

Residential v commercial

We have discussed the residential property investment sector at some length, but commercial property can be an excellent addition to a healthy investment portfolio if you are looking for consistent, steady yields alongside a decent level of growth.

Commercial real estate has shown long-term positive performance, with combined annual returns averaging around 9% depending on the area and type of property.

The steady and predictable cash stream potentially afforded by rental income from commercial property translates to possible protection against volatility in financial markets.

Here are some reasons why investors may find commercial property attractive

- Historically strong returns – with an average annual return of about 9% over a 20-year period commercial real estate has performed well historically.
- Rental income from stable commercial properties means a potential steady and predictable cash stream (translating into possible protection and diversification during financial market volatility).
- Beneficial taxation – when structured properly, commercial property can offer investors a number of tax benefits.
- A hedge against inflation – a potentially important factor for your portfolio, since property normally benefits from inflation.

- Ability to leverage your capital – as with residential property you can obtain mortgages and potentially multiply your ROCE (return on capital employed).
- Diversification – there is no direct correlation with the stock market and you can further diversify within the asset class itself.

These are some of the different types of commercial property into which you can invest and spread your risk:

- office property (either prime or secondary);
- industrial property: warehouse and manufacturing units; heavy manufacturing; light assembly; 'flex' warehouses (mixed industrial/office space); and bulk warehouses, like distribution centres.;
- retail: individual shops, take-aways, shopping centres, etc.;
- multi-unit apartment buildings/HMOs: although providing homes, these are treated as commercial premises;
- self-storage: self-contained units rented to tenants for storage of material items, usually on a monthly basis;
- hotels: bed and breakfast, small boutique hotels or big-name establishments.

However, property investors when they start investing seem to prefer residential, perhaps understandably, as it falls more easily within their knowledge base and comfort zone.

The philosophical difference between residential and commercial is that when you invest in residential property, you are essentially transacting with individuals – it is a much more personal transaction especially as people will be living in your property and making it their home.

On the other hand, when dealing with commercial property the position is much more business-like and impersonal as you are essentially dealing with commercial entities and everything is negotiated by lawyers. If, for example, the rent is not paid on the due date, the contract will stipulate a series of remedies that can quickly be enforced. If the property is not maintained to certain contractually agreed standards, then the owner can remedy the position and require the tenant to pay the bill.

In general terms, there are numerous regulations regarding the letting of residential property to individuals which overrule anything you may wish to put in your rental agreement. These regulations may prevent you from evicting people even if they have not paid their rent or if they cause serious damage to the property.

On the other hand, commercial leases normally have a clause in the back that stipulates should you pay the rent late than penalty interest will accrue and be applied to the amount of rent outstanding. Additionally, if the rents have still not been paid after a certain period of time then the landlord will have the right to not only change the locks but seize all the tenant's fittings, furniture and equipment and may sell them in order to recover any rent due. There some regulations governing this, but by and large, your remedies as a commercial landlord are far greater than those of a residential landlord.

In general, therefore, you will have much greater flexibility with the terms you can agree with commercial property.

With regard to commercial property, tenants usually derive their income from the business carried out at the premises. Therefore, they have a vested interest in keeping the property well maintained. Bearing that in mind, you can usually expect your tenants to keep the property well maintained and they will quite often even improve it at their own expense.

Unfortunately, with residential property, there is rarely the same motivation to maintain the property, and it is even more unlikely that they will want to improve the premises, especially at their own cost. Although I have encountered instances of my tenants decorating prem-ises in their own style, it usually does not fit the definition of 'improving a property'. Creating a purple mural of Jimi Hendrix (as one tenant chose to do) definitely didn't add value to my property.

The point to grasp is that the fundamental mentality is very different. If something goes wrong with the commercial premises the tenants will want to fix it immediately as it directly affects them and their business. They know that they are normally obligated to undertake these repairs in any event. However, the attitude of most residential tenancies is that whatever goes wrong is the landlord's responsibility. This includes situations where they have gone out and got drunk on a Saturday night, lost the key and think it perfectly reasonable to call the landlord in the middle of the night to help. I have learned the hard way and always turn my phone off before I go to bed. After all, I am their landlord, not their father.

It is clear that despite what you may have read about property being a passive income, it's rarely the case, especially as your portfolio grows. And once you have 20 or so residential properties, it becomes very time consuming. Alternatively, commercial properties are a lot less demanding. Tenants tend to do minor repairs themselves, turnover is not as high since leases last for a number of years and many businesses will choose to renew.

Length of lease.

A major difference between residential and commercial property is in the typical lease period.

Residential property is usually governed by an AST (Assured Shorthold Tenancy) which is typically for six or 12 months. After that, it usually reverts to a periodic tenancy whereby any party can give notice – usually one month.

By contrast, commercial properties are generally for many years at a time. For example, The House Crowd had to commit to a three-year period when it rented its offices. Leases with much longer terms are common.

Business want stability and a long lease is generally desirable for both parties as it gives each the security they require. It is not uncommon to see leases of 20 years or more with commercial property. Conversely with residential properties, tenants often want flexibility, and tying them into something longer term is undesirable as it reduces their freedom to move house.

Acquiring tenants

In respect of residential property, once the tenant leaves, that is usually the end of your relationship with that tenant. Certainly, if they fail to pay the rent, you are not able to go back to the previous tenants and ask him or her to make up the shortfall. However, the situation is very different with commercial property. You can grant a long-term lease to a commercial tenant and if they wish to move on before the expiry of that lease, they will remain liable for the rent. Should the company to whom your tenant sublets fail to pay the rent, the original tenant will normally still be liable to you. That is why commercial properties with strong covenants and strong healthy tenant companies are highly regarded.

Most commercial leases will also prevent the sale of the business without landlord approval as it would give the tenant too easy a way to absolve themselves of their contractual obligations.

Void periods

It's clear that commercial properties do have many advantages over residential. However, the biggest advantage of residential over commercial is when a lease comes to an end.

Whilst void periods certainly occur with residential property, if you bought a property in an area with strong rental demand, there is usually only one reason why the property will remain empty: the rent you are asking is too high.

Conversely, you may have a commercial property that has nothing wrong with it but can stand vacant for years on end – even if the rent is slashed. The reason for this is that commercial property can be much more specialised and you may be restricted to a particular sort of tenant for the property.

Commercial property is also much more vulnerable to economic downturns or other factors that have changed the economy; just look around many town centres, even reasonably affluent ones, where there are numerous retail outlets that have not been used for many years due to changes in people's buying patterns. The same is now happening with out-of-town retail parks as online shopping has decimated their revenue stream.

So which is best for you?

Whether you invest in residential, commercial or both is a decision for you to make.

Investing in residential is pretty straightforward – everybody knows what a home looks like and can exercise their judgement fairly easily as to whether it is a suitable property to let.

Investing in commercial property requires more specialist knowledge and can be a little daunting. There is a much wider variety of properties and factors that must be taken into account. It is therefore more difficult for beginners to know what commercial tenants will want and to select properties accordingly.

Probably the biggest advantage of commercial property is that if you are ambitious and want to build up a multi-million-pound portfolio it is a lot easier to find and manage a small number of commercial properties that may be worth £30 million than it is to find and manage £30 million worth of residential property.

Residential vs commercial summary

Residential
- Rents are quoted monthly.
- Tenants have little interest in improving the property or maintaining it well.
- Leases are generally for six months only.
- Tenants will expect you to deal with minor problems.
- The government and the council legislate the area heavily in order to protect the rights of tenants.
- The capital required to buy is generally lower, as high loan to value mortgages are available.
- If the property is empty, it is relatively easy to find a new tenant.
- The management time involved can be onerous.

Commercial
- Rentals are quoted annually.
- Tenants have a vested interest in keeping the property looking good and improving it.
- Leases tend to be for a number of years.
- Tenants will tend to fix minor problems and may be contracted to do all repairs.
- There is less bureaucratic interference.
- Capital needed to purchase is usually greater and banks generally only lend up to 50% of the valuation.
- Often the appraisal value is based upon the rental income being received and considerable uplifts in value can be achieved if a higher rent can be obtained.

- With empty properties it may be difficult to find a new tenant and the property could be vacant for years.
- Time spent on management is minimal.

I can certainly see the advantages in commercial property but, for a variety of personal preferences and my own circumstances, I have always focused on residential property and the rest of the book deals solely with residential property investment.

Chapter 7

How to beat the averages and give yourself the best chance of making a successful property investment

Let's consider a geographical region in which the average yield is around 4%. Many investors may take those average yields at face value, and accept that this is the amount they can expect from investment in property within that region. However, it is important to note that averages are not set in stone, and are not necessarily indicative of what can be achieved within that market, provided, that is, the investor is sufficiently informed and knowledgeable enough to tip the balance in his favour.

With this in mind, it is possible to greatly increase the average returns for your investment property within an area. But, it is not an easy win. Firstly, you must ask yourself what your chances are, realistically, of beating those averages. It involves research and learning, but ultimately, I believe it is substantially easier than beating the average gains achievable by investing in stocks and shares which are considerably more complex.

Two principal questions to ask yourself in order to establish your chances of success:

1. How much does the investment sector in which I am investing fluctuate around its average?

2. How much does each specific investment within a sector fluctuate around the sector average?

By comparing share market growth against property market growth over the last 50 years, you will notice that both have grown by an average of 8%. However, despite this parallel, there are significant differences that belie any apparent equivalence between the two. By looking at the figures, it's plain to see that the average stock market price has fluctuated to a much greater extent over that period, whilst the trajectory of property market growth demonstrates more of a steady incline.

From this evidence, we can ascertain that, whatever property you buy, it is likely to see increases by approximately the average for properties in that geographical area over an extended period of time. There is significantly less certainty on the stock market.

Property market prices rise in unison, as a result of general market forces. If a property is priced too highly, it will be less appealing to buyers, who will ultimately opt for one which conforms closer to the average market value.

Stocks and shares, on the other hand, rise and fall within their own bubble. In a market where 4,999 shares rise by 10%, there are no guarantees that the 5,000th will do so. As such, reading averages in order to pick stock market investments is not a reliable course of action, whereas, with property, it is.

However, that said, when it comes to property investment, it's not hard to beat the average statistics, just by applying a bit of knowledge and common sense.

Here are a few key factors to consider.

Location and price growth opportunities
As we have seen in previous chapters, property prices vary from location to location. The average national growth may be 7%, but within that average some areas fell or remained flat, others flourished far above that figure, and others were more closely aligned to the overall average.

This equates to a necessity to seek out and invest in those areas which are flourishing above the average. In today's UK property market, for example, Manchester and Leeds are two areas that exceed the average rates of growth whilst in London, Dalston is currently thriving but Chelsea and Belgravia have seen a fall in property values over the last six months.

Regeneration

It is not only by investing in already-flourishing areas, however, that you will find the best yields. Investment in areas that are undergoing regeneration can also be a judicious choice.

You can easily spot local upcoming areas by the emergence of the nicer supermarkets and the growth of the more upmarket restaurant chains.

Visiting local council websites is another great way to learn about regeneration plans. These will have details of plans for new amenities, shopping centres, transport links, investment in new housing. All these are key indicators of probable property market growth.

Large employers moving to an area are also another reliable indicator. These companies undertake significant research and spend a lot of money on ascertaining where they should open new branches. They will ultimately choose those where their research demonstrates increasing affluence. You don't necessarily need direct access to the research itself. By simply keeping your eyes open to see which companies are moving to an area, you can generally predict that average capital growth and increased rent will be imminent, or already underway.

It isn't difficult to distinguish which businesses work within this model. You will see old pubs being replaced by trendy bars and 'gastropubs'. Restaurant chains tied to particular demographics, and supermarkets, are also good indicators. One commonly repeated sign to look out for is the Waitrose effect: wherever there is a new Waitrose, it is said, there is money to be made in property.

And, of course, with large employers comes an increased population which may lead to an imbalance of supply and demand in accommodation for those who work there.

Local goldmines

As we have already established, there is no single UK property market to speak of.

Even within specific towns themselves, there can be widely disparate rates of growth between different areas. You will need to narrow your search down to the level of individual neighbourhoods in order to identify the best opportunities – the real goldmines.

Areas that have historically seen the best growth rates in house price values are generally the most desirable areas in town, so focus on those if it's long-term capital growth you want.

However, if you are looking for rental yields, the converse is often true, and the cheaper areas tend to produce the highest yields. Research areas carefully to identify the hidden buy-to-let goldmines in your town. These will be where the rents are much higher in proportion to the cost of the property. They exist in every single town – you just need to know where to look.

This is one of our key focuses at The House Crowd. We spend a great deal of time researching all possible areas within a half-hour radius in order to ascertain the best price-to-rent achievable ratio: pockets where the housing stock is lower in price, but the rents are equal to those in surrounding areas.

We focus largely on cash flow-generating properties, so after considering many areas, our research led us to settle on just four small areas in the whole of Manchester that offered the best opportunities for buying properties which would deliver the highest yields.

The 'overspill' factor

The 'overspill' factor is another relevant metric to take into account. If I can add a personal example here, this may serve best to illustrate the point.

When I first moved to London, in 1994, I was looking for a flat in Camden. I was unable to find a desirable property within my budget at that time. However, looking just up the road in Kentish Town, I was able to find a nice flat which I could afford. Over time, others identified the same issue, and over the next few years, Kentish Town increased in popularity, prices rose considerably, and the area has become a much smarter, more coveted postcode.

Demographics

Understanding patterns and shifts within the population of a given area, and applying that knowledge wisely, is another key way to beat the average returns.

At present, due to several factors – including property affordability – most people are renting for longer, often into their thirties. This is a good indicator that the market for reasonably priced one-bedroom flats is likely to rise.

The older generation of 'baby boomers' are fast approaching retirement age. In fact, the news of our ageing population is widely known. This means there is an increased need for retirement homes, and the demand for those is growing rapidly.

As such, areas where the population is ageing rapidly are likely to see better than average growth and within those areas retirement home properties are likely to prove an even better investment.

Living by the sea

Since the industrial revolution, and principally within the last 100 years, we have seen increased migration to cities. This is where the work is. And in the last 15 years, city centres themselves have become an increasingly popular choice to live in for people who wish to be near the action – the nightlife, the restaurants, the shopping, and ultimately others of their peer group. Cities are where young professionals find the most enriching lives, and the numbers living in city centre populations are certainly forecast to increase over the next decade.

Conversely, as people get older, their interests change. They seek out a more peaceful life for themselves. In addition, as the power of the internet has grown, so too have the opportunities for remote working. Rather than being limited to where their office is located, people can now essentially work anywhere they wish. And without the need to travel to work each day, comes the freedom to also live wherever they wish.

And the simple fact is that given a choice, most people would choose to live by the sea, especially if it's only a couple of hours' commute to the office a few times a month.

Expect demand for coastal property to increase over the next decade.

Property types

If you cross-reference what you've learned about the most promising areas, key target demographics, and so on, against the type of properties that are likely to see the best returns, you will probably come up with two options.

Terraced properties are popular choices for renters, achieving higher rental yields than flats.

Flats have the downside of service charges. These are rarely good value for money, and are often excessively high. These service charges will have an impact on your rental returns, and thus make them a less appealing investment opportunity.

If you are focused on the highest yields and capital growth, there is a surprising forerunner. The bungalow.

Returning to our findings about the ageing population, there is a promising overlap between the demand for bungalows in this demographic. Renting to older tenants comes with fewer hassles than with younger tenants, and anecdotal evidence confirms, at least to me, that those investing in this area of the buy-to-let sector can see excellent returns.

From the points detailed above, it is therefore possible to hypothesise that the ultimate investment property could be a rundown bungalow, on the best street in a seaside town that is undergoing a significant regeneration programme and is within an hour's commute of a thriving city.

Such a property may be a rare find indeed. But by simply applying a few of the factors above, you should be able to ensure your investment beats the so-called average returns.

Chapter summary

Factors to consider when making an investment decision if you want to beat average returns include:

- location, location, location
- investment in the local infrastructure
- identifying local goldmines that provide better yields
- the overspill factor
- the changing nature of the population and how people live
- the type of property.

Chapter 8

The UK property market – 2017 and beyond

The buy-to-let market in the UK really gained traction in 1996, with the opening of the buy-to-let mortgage market. This made property investment accessible to millions who could now obtain buy-to-let mortgages whilst putting down only relatively small deposits.

It proved immensely popular, and many people found the idea of property as a means to provide a retirement income preferable to putting their money in a traditional pension.

However, after many years of encouraging people to invest in buy-to-let property, over the last two years, the government has ruthlessly stabbed buy-to-let investors in the back and has crippled the ability of small landlords to make any sort of decent profit.

The attack has been so brutal that many, including one of Britain's largest private landlords, Fergus Wilson, has claimed that buy-to-let is dead.

Not only has there been an ever-creeping amount of red tape and financial burden placed upon landlords in recent years, and George Osbourne, in 2015, saw fit to increase stamp duty on the purchase of second properties directly targeting landlords who he misguidedly views as part of Britain's housing problem.

Then, in an astonishingly cynical and highly discriminatory move, he decreed that landlords should be treated differently from every other type of UK business and would no longer be able to offset loan interest payments against revenue. From April 2017, Interest Relief Restriction will restrict the tax relief that residential property investors receive on their mortgage interest and other finance costs. As the expenses allowed are cut, landlords' rental profits, for the purposes of taxation only, will (artificially) increase. The changes will be introduced in four equal stages, from 2017 through to 2020.

The government has created a corresponding tax credit of 20% of the interest cost, to offset this and reduce the landlord's tax bill, claiming that it will make the change self-cancelling for landlords who are basic rate taxpayers. However, the tax credit will not be sufficient to fully offset the tax liabilities of higher rate tax payers. Not only that, but there is the fact that the change to profit calculation will push many of those who currently fall into the basic rate bracket into a higher tax bracket as it artificially increases their taxable profits.

It is, therefore, pretty certain that the only landlords who will not suffer are those on low incomes with small portfolios. Most professional landlords will, inevitably, end up paying more tax on amounts that are significantly greater than the true amount of profit.

What this means for the large majority of landlords who have buy-to-let mortgages and do not operate under a limited company structure, is that they will incur heavy losses and could, potentially, be forced into bankruptcy, as their tax bill could exceed their true profit from rental income. The National Landlord Association believes it will have a severely detrimental effect on 44% of landlords. Unfortunately, research indicates only a small percentage of landlords are aware of this cataclysmic change and the effect it will have.

On top of that, Chancellor Philip Hammond recently announced legislation to prevent letting agents charging fees to tenants. This will doubtless put a further financial burden on landlords as letting agents look to charge them the fees instead for credit and reference checks. Landlords may be able to put up rents to an extent to counteract this but the situation in Scotland showed that there was a very limited cap on how much increase the market could stand.

The Bank of England has also implemented strict new rules which adversely affect landlords. Concerned about the exposure of certain banks to the buy-to-let market, the Bank of England has ruled that lenders must apply much stricter criteria to landlords looking to borrow. These rules mean that landlords, in many cases, will not be able to get mortgages they would otherwise have been able to and, if they can, they will find them considerably more expensive.

It's no wonder that an industry report, published at the end of 2016, showed that, in the year to November, buy-to-let sales fell by 64%. Simultaneously, the number of landlords who registered to buy a new investment property fell by 59%.

It seems clear to me that the traditional way of investing in buy-to-let property – as an individual putting down a 20% deposit and taking out a buy-to-let mortgage – that has thrived over the last 20 years, and provided many with the hope of a better retirement income, is no longer the clear winner it once was.

Property, though, despite all this, seems destined to remain the nation's favourite asset class. However, the types of property and the way people invest in it will need to change. Crowdfunding, as we shall see, is probably the best, and perhaps the only, way individual investors can still access this asset class profitably.

The government has now thrown its support behind 'build to rent' and the PRS. PRS refers to the private rental sector and usually to purpose-built blocks owned by institutions – generally with a high standard of communal facilities designed to attract and keep tenants long term.

Large urban developments are being financed by institutional funds and managed by large companies to cater for Generation Rent. For example, the government has announced that £45 million of its new £3 billion Home Building Fund will go towards kick-starting a deal involving 2,000 new build-to-rent homes including 995 purpose-built units in Manchester. Combined with the recent attacks on buy-to-let, it is likely that this will consolidate build-to-rent as the future of rented living and property investment in Britain.

Given the scale of the developments, and the money required to finance them, it is clearly not something readily accessible to individual investors. The only way individual investors can really benefit from direct investment in such large schemes is through crowdfunding and peer-to-peer secured lending platforms which enable them to earn returns on par with institutional investors.

Chapter summary

- Why traditional buy-to-let investing is no longer profitable.
- Loss of government support for buy-to-let.
- Increasing tax and regulatory burdens.
- Changes in government housing policy.
- Policy shift towards supporting large institutions and build-to-rent sector.

Chapter 9

Passive property investment

The main drawback of property, as we touched on earlier, is the time and effort it takes to invest and manage a portfolio. But there are now several ways you can invest passively in property, without getting your hands dirty.

Your main options are, apart from investing in shares of house builders and other property companies, REITs or alternative finance platforms offering debt (peer-to-peer lending) or equity (shares) based crowdfunding.

Let's deal with REITs first.

REITs, or real estate investment trusts, are companies that own investment properties. They can provide a good option for gaining exposure to the real estate sector. REIT shares are listed on a stock exchange and can be purchased and sold in the same way as other types of stock. Traditionally, they tend to hold a range of different kinds of real estate, including both residential and commercial properties.

Similar to mutual funds, REITs pool investments together, generate capital gains and investment income, and allow investors to choose investments from a diversified portfolio of assets.

Although both REITs and crowdfunding offer ways to access property, they are very different beasts indeed. We compare REITS with property crowdfunding at the end of this chapter but here's a quick summary of the benefits and drawbacks of REITs.

The pros
- Large pay-outs can result in above average yields, which is a primary consideration for dividend investors.
- As real estate values are separate from stock prices, their values can move either in completely opposite directions, or together. As such, creating a diverse portfolio which contains both real estate holdings and other stocks, will complement each other: providing protection against any slumps in one or the other asset class.
- At least 90% of the income from a REIT must be paid out in dividends. REIT managers can raise pay-outs over the 90% mark, but are legally forbidden to lower it below that amount. This is probably the main reason for investors to choose REITs as an investment.
- Compared to standard real estate investments, REITs offer higher liquidity. To cash out, you simply sell your shares, whereas with a whole property investment, you would have to sell the property.
- Like property crowdfunding, REITs allow you to avoid the costs and hassles of a traditional property investment. Even better, you don't even need to find and research the properties, as this is taken care of by the REIT's managers.
- REITs allow you to own a tangible asset, which tends to rise in value in the long term.
- Again, like property crowdfunding, REITs make it easy to create a diverse property portfolio. Money is pooled from a group of investors, which allows the REIT to buy more buildings than you'd be able to buy on your own. This diversification mitigates risk, as if one of the properties in the portfolio starts under-performing, you will still have the others to fall back on. Also, your money is not locked up in one building.

The cons
- There are risks involved in any kind of investment, and REITs are subject to the same risks associated with other kinds of real estate, or stock investing.
- If property prices fall, so will the value of your shares.
- Interest rate rises will negatively affect profitability.

- Based on the supply and demand ratio of shares, prices of REIT shares can fall along with the broader stock market.
- Revenues can be affected by vacant periods on a property.
- Though some REIT dividends qualify for 15% tax rates, others are taxed as ordinary income.

As with any kind of investment you're considering, you need to weigh up all factors and make a decision that's going to be right for you. When it comes to taxes, it is prudent to consult a tax specialist to ascertain what the net effect on your tax bill is going to be, before you invest.

How do REITS compare with property crowdfunding?

The key differences between crowdfunding and REITs are the level of liquidity, the amount of control and where you, as an investor, sit in the value chain.

Firstly, the positive of REITs is that they are liquid and people can get in and out quickly. Crowdfunding, at present, only has a limited secondary market, so it is only marginally more liquid than any individual property investment. This may be a positive or negative thing depending on your point of view.

Secondly, the reality of REITS is that they do not produce results that compare favourably with direct property investment. The main reason for this is the number of intermediaries involved and the (exorbitant) fees they charge.

The first step in the life cycle of a property is acquiring suitable land and gaining planning permission. This usually leads to an uplift of around 30% in the value of the land. A developer will then buy the land with planning permission and build the authorised offices, houses or apartments on it. His profit margin will typically be between 15–25%.

The buyer (which may well be the same party as the developer) then buys the asset and looks to increase the value by tenanting the property. This is called 'seasoning the rents'. The investor is usually looking for a 20% return on their money. They receive their money by selling the asset to a REIT that is looking to increase the amount of rental income it has under management. The REIT is essentially trying to acquire cashflow so that it can pay the monthly contributions to investors in the REIT and it typically looks for yields of 5–8%. This trust or fund then has to be regulated and managed, both of which eat into the returns further.

The average REIT can have as many as 16 different fees involved.

The last person in this value chain after all the profit taking and fee making and regulatory costs is you – the investor – which, simply put, is why nobody becomes wealthy by investing in REITs.

The best way to get wealthy in property is via direct investment. As we know, there used to be significant barriers to entry in doing so but the fact is, if you want to achieve better results from investing you need to invest higher up the value chain. Crowdfunding enables you to do so by investing in property directly, albeit with some fees to pay.

A vital point to understand is that, unlike REITS, property crowd-funding is not a financial instrument. You are investing directly into prop-erty. This makes a big difference. Whilst I will readily acknowledge that direct property investment is susceptible to market sentiment and that values can fluctuate, it is unarguable that the property market is consider-ably more stable than the stock market. REITs have a 70%–80% correla-tion with the stock market and whilst some people may look on them as a way to access property as an asset class, they are in fact almost as vola-tile as the stock market and are, therefore, not providing true diversity.

The wealthiest members of society tend to invest in property directly, and via crowdfunding it is now open to a much broader segment of society to do so.

A final note: the new alternative finance platforms do away with the murky world of funds and REITS, where you are never sure where your money is being invested or what fees are being charged. The technology provides a high level of transparency – you know exactly what you are investing in, what your returns should be and what fees are being made.

Chapter summary

- Fact: property management is time intensive and often emotion-ally draining.
- Why passive investing makes sense.
- Why you will never get rich investing in REITs.

Chapter 10

A brief history of the alternative finance industry

It is often said that the internet has been the most democratising invention of modern times. It has transformed how we communicate, how we buy, how we live and how we do business. It has also completely revolutionised how we invest.

Crowdfunding itself is nothing new. It was first used, in fact, back in the 19th century, when newspaper publisher Joseph Pulitzer appealed to the public for donations for the erection of the Statue of Liberty in New York. In exchange, those who donated received either a six- or twelve-inch statue, depending on how much they had offered.

But it was not until relatively recently that the internet enabled fundraisers access to much greater numbers of potential investors and opened the doors to a whole new way of financing projects. The combining of scepticism of the big banks after the financial crisis, low interest rates, and the emerging new technologies created the perfect melting pot for the exponential rise of the alternative finance industry. It's an industry that encompasses fintech (tech companies offering financial products and services), proptech (tech companies operating in the property space), peer-to-peer lending – both secured and unsecured, reward-based crowdfunding – often used for artistic projects, and equity crowdfunding in businesses (often start-ups or early stage companies) and notably in property, which is now the largest single sector.

Crowdfunding benefits both sides of the equation.

It gives retail investors opportunities to help finance projects they support and gives them access to investments from which they were traditionally excluded, either because of regulations, lack of contacts or access to the levels of capital previously required. And, through crowdfunding, SMEs have found new ways to finance their businesses, creatives have found new ways to fund their projects, and charities have found a new mechanism for increasing donations. And when the first property crowdfunding platform, The House Crowd, arrived on the scene in 2012, the face of property investment changed forever.

It was only through making use of narrow exemptions in the Financial Services and Markets Act that The House Crowd was able to start trading legally in March 2012. It wasn't long before others began following suit, and the industry really began to take off.

In 2016, in the UK, the entire alternative finance sector surpassed the £5 billion mark. Property crowdfunding is the most popular sector within the alternative finance market and, globally, is forecast to grow to US$250 billion per year by 2020.

In the UK, in 2015, combined debt (peer-to-peer) and equity-based property crowdfunding was valued at close to £700 million, and continues to grow rapidly. Peer-to-peer lending in the real estate sector accounted for £609 million of this, and accounted for 41% of the total volume of peer-to-peer business loans in 2015. The remaining £87 million came from equity crowdfunding.

The continued success of the alternative finance industry has been, in some part, aided by government support. In 2015, the British Business Bank lent £60 million through peer-to-peer lending platforms, and the government has created an Innovative Finance ISA that allows investments to be made via a peer-to-peer platform to be held in a tax efficient ISA wrapper. Lending platforms believe the IFISA will lead to a 51.9% growth in transactional volume over the course of 2018.

Institutional investment in the alternative finance industry has also rocketed. In 2015, 45% of all alternative finance platforms received institutional involvement, up from 28% in 2014. In property based platforms specifically, the figure was 25%.

Recent research has found that nearly half of retail investors would like to increase their exposure to the UK property market through investment via peer-to-peer platforms.

By removing the time and fees involved in owning an entire property as an investment, more and more people are now ready, willing and able to get involved in property investment.

Alternative finance, in short, has become an integral part of the development of a whole new range of financial products. Whilst traditional financial institutions are tied up in outdated processes that are keeping them from engaging with the new digital innovations that the internet has allowed, the alternative finance industry has been free to create an entirely new landscape for our financial lives.

Chapter summary

- The internet has disrupted many industries.
- Crowdfunding is nothing new – it started way back in the 19th century.
- The first property crowdfunding site was launched in 2012.
- Crowdfunding has democratised property investment.
- The property crowdfunding market is already worth billions and is set to grow to US$250 billion by the end of 2020.

Chapter 11

All about equity crowdfunding

Both peer-to-peer secured lending and property crowdfunding are regulated by the Financial Conduct Authority (FCA), and you should ensure any site you use is appropriately authorised to operate.

You should also note that neither type of platform is covered by the Financial Services Compensation Scheme (FSCS) (except when money is being held in a regulated bank account), meaning there is no government bailout should the platform or the projects you invest in run into financial difficulties. However, all responsible platforms will have plans in place to ringfence individual investments and contingency plans for the continued administration of the platform and return of capital to investors should the company fail.

On the plus side, both models offer the opportunity for higher returns than you would receive from investments in which your money (up to £75,000) was fully protected by the FSCS. Every investment will have its own inherent risks and its own level of security, so it really is a personal choice for you to make depending on what level of risk you are comfortable with.

Equity crowdfunding provides the potential for very high returns when the businesses invested in are either floated successfully or sold at a high multiple to earnings. However, it's a fact that many start-ups do fail, some misuse investor funds and even if they do well, it doesn't necessarily mean you, as a shareholder, will make a huge profit. You should invest very carefully and never invest with money you cannot afford to lose.

One reason why investors find property crowdfunding so attractive is that, whilst it doesn't perhaps carry the excitement of investing in a new company with a revolutionary product, it does offer a solid investment secured by the bricks and mortar value of the property and a simple, easy-to-understand business model showing how it is intended that money will be made.

That's not to say things can't go wrong – they do from time to time – but given that the land and property will always have some value, the risk of losing a large part of your money is significantly less than investing in a start-up company. Some of the situations we have encountered (or just heard about) that negatively affect forecast returns include: void periods/non-payment of rent, legal fees to evict tenants, damage to the property/unforeseen maintenance, tenants suing for some type of injury incurred on the premises, changes in legislation/taxation, Brexit, changes in rental market conditions, general decline in the property market, Compulsory Purchase Orders, HS2 (or similar) being built close to your property, insurance premiums escalating, etc.

So, if you are considering investing, you must do so with the understanding that *all* investments, including property-based ones (whether investing individually or via crowdfunding), do involve risk and it is always wise to mitigate that risk with a properly diversified portfolio.

Chapter summary

- Companies must be FCA regulated to operate legally.
- FSCS protects up to £75,000 only whilst money is held in regulated bank accounts.
- Platforms make money on successfully raising funds for third parties.
- The accreditation process required before you are legally allowed to invest.
- The benefits of crowdfunding.

How do crowdfunding platforms make money?

In respect of equity crowdfunding most platforms will make money in two ways.

Firstly, they will charge the companies raising funds a fee based on the monies raised – this is typically 5%. That means that in the case of property purchases the companies being promoted (i.e. those raising money) need to raise 5% more in fees than an individual would need in finance to purchase that property and, consequently, the gross return will be reduced by approximately 5%.

Additionally, the platforms will charge a fee for the ongoing management of the asset – typically 10–15% of the rent collected/profit on sale.

In respect of peer-to-peer (debt) investments, fees are usually charged to the borrower rather than the investors who should receive the publicised rate.

The process of investing

Most property crowdfunding platforms offer very similar processes and investing is usually simple and straightforward.

Firstly, it is important to note that the FCA have stipulated that before you can even access specific information about investments through a crowdfunding platform, you need to register with the site and the platform needs to ensure you are suitably qualified to invest.

To qualify you must fit into one of these categories:

- a high net worth investor
- a sophisticated investor
- an advised investor (i.e. you have received advice from a qualified financial adviser)
- a crowdfunding investor.

The site will provide legal definitions of each category.

If you fall within the definition of one of the first three categories, you can self-certify that you do so, but you may be asked for supporting evidence.

As far as the crowdfunding investor category is concerned, you must answer a basic questionnaire to illustrate that you understand the investments listed and the inherent risks. You will also need to certify that you are not investing more than 10% of your net assets in crowdfunding.

Before you can invest, you will also need to provide, for anti-money laundering purposes, appropriate identification.

With equity crowdfunding you will be investing in shares in a company set up with the sole purpose of buying the relevant property. It's referred to as an SPV (single purpose vehicle).

The platform will list the available investments together with all pertinent legal and financial information.

You can select the properties you wish to invest in and, when you have done so, you transfer funds using a bank transfer or debit card via an e-wallet system. The e-wallet provider will hold your money in a segregated and regulated client account until the property purchase is made. During this time, it is protected up to £75,000 in each individual case by the FSCS.

Some platforms allow you to invest with as little as £50, but the minimum is usually £1,000 or more. Once the funding has reached the required level, the property will be purchased.

Following purchase, you will either receive your share certificates in your name or they will be held for you by the platform's trustee (which enables an easier transfer should you wish to sell them).

Dividends should be paid in accordance with the website's policy provided there is sufficient profit from the rent to do so and the property will be sold as per the relevant investment information provided. Investors share in any profits on sale pro rata.

Most platforms offer an online account where you can see the properties you have invested in and track their progress. You should also be able to view all relevant legal and financial information pertaining to your properties. But other than that, there is no need for you to do anything – the SPV manages the asset and deals with all the property or tenant-related issues that arise on behalf of all shareholders.

True passive property investment.

Chapter 12

How does property crowdfunding compare with traditional property investment?

Investing as an individual in buy-to-let property, as we have seen in earlier chapters, may no longer be feasible for most people. To do so profitably you would probably need to set up and purchase through a limited company and be able to put down deposits of at least 40% to generate a decent cashflow.

There are of course other models for property investing such as refurbishing or converting properties to sell or developing new-build property. However, for an individual, these are even more time consuming than buy-to-let and more akin to businesses than passive investments.

If you are a professional property investor with access to capital, then you are unlikely to be reading this book and it is even more unlikely there will be much benefit in crowdfunding for you. You will have many advantages such as access to funding, first-hand knowledge and experience, your own contacts for sourcing deals and carrying out works, control over who you rent to and when you decide to sell ... and you will be able to keep all the profits yourself. If you are in that enviable position, then there probably isn't much that crowdfunding can do to help you.

However, there are many disgruntled landlords – people who are fed up with the increasing burden placed upon them by government, weary of dealing with tenants and their multitude of problems and dismayed by decreasing profits – who are turning to crowdfunding as an easier method of investing. If you fall into this category, are new to property investment, or simply want a completely passive property investment, then there are a host of reasons why it may make sense for you to invest in property through crowdfunding.

Here is a quick recap of the recent changes that have made buy-to-let considerably less attractive for individual investors over the last few years:

- increased mandatory licensing by councils imposing extra costs and administration;
- increased health and safety legislation imposing extra costs and administration;
- increased environmental regulations imposing extra costs and administration;
- an extra 3% stamp duty on second properties/properties bought through a limited company;
- interest relief restriction;
- ban on letting agents charging fees to tenants;
- tightening of criteria on buy-to-let mortgages;
- rise of build-to-rent/purpose-built student accommodation;
- increase in level of deposit required.

Crowdfunding cannot completely mitigate all these issues but it does mitigate several of them and has many other advantages over individual investing.

Spreading risk

One of the main advantages of crowdfunding is that it enables you to spread whatever available money you have over a larger number of investments, thus avoiding putting all your eggs in one basket. Things, as I have pointed out, can go wrong and it's clearly preferable to have a tenant not paying rent in one of ten properties you have a share in, than the tenant in the only property you own not paying rent.

Hands-free investing

The passive nature of crowdfunding is also very appealing to those who use crowdfunding platforms. As a property investor, you may have to deal with all sorts of issues – everything from incompetent solicitors, lazy mortgage brokers, banks, estate agents, subsidence, Japanese knotweed infestation, troublesome tenants, and fire and flood damage. In short, there are frequent problems and the larger your portfolio the more of a full-time occupation it can become. Crowdfunding removes all of that as the properties are all professionally managed on behalf of all investors and you simply get to read about the problems in the reports the crowdfunding platform (should) produce for you.

Expertise

The vetting of a potential investment by experienced property people also reduces the chances of you, as an amateur investor, buying a lemon; though, admittedly, it doesn't stop it altogether as there are some things that just cannot be foreseen.

Lower financial burden/risk

Leverage can help increase profits when investing in property. Conversely, it also increases risk as you are vulnerable to interest rate increases and must still make the mortgage payments when the property is empty. This can lead to you having to subsidise your investments and in many cases, after 2007, led to bankruptcy for people who had over-stretched themselves.

With crowdfunding, leverage in the form of borrowing is rarely used – though some platforms use a moderate level of borrowing. What you are doing is leveraging the crowd's money by pooling resources. Whilst profits need to be shared proportionately it considerably lowers the risk inherent in property investing and, while unpaid rent may undermine the return you were expecting, at least there will be no call to make that month's mortgage payment. And, most importantly, there is no chance of a property being repossessed if there is no borrowing against it.

Here's a table showing a comparison of traditional buy-to-let investing as an individual investing versus crowdfunding.

Factor	Buy on your own	Invest via crowdfunding
Control	You will have greater control as an individual investor	Reliant on directors of SPV to make decisions and may require shareholders' majority to sell the property
Share of profits	You keep all profits after repayment of finance	Profits of both rental income and capital appreciation are shared pro rata
Leverage	Borrowing at attractive rates can massively increase profits but also increases risk. Benefits of borrowing have been undermined by interest relief reductions	Leveraging of pooled resources enables more purchases and risk mitigation but profits will be shared pro rata
Taxation	Depending on individual circumstances	Can receive £5,000 in dividend income tax free each year
Time and effort required to find a suitable property	Considerable time and effort required	Very little time required to select pre-vetted investments
Buy regularly and get access to the best deals	Unlikely unless you are a large-scale professional investor	Platforms should have buying power and strong relationships with estate agents and receivers
Thorough due diligence undertaken	You rely on your own skill and experience to avoid costly mistakes	Property professionals vet all investments reducing the chances of a bad investment
Legal fees	You pay all fees – likely to be at least £1,000	You pay a small fraction
Survey fees	You pay all – likely to be at least £300	You pay a small fraction
Find and manage reliable builders	You need to do and it can be problematical	SPV will project manage everything
Spend time and money to find tenants/deal with letting agents	Can be expensive and time consuming	The SPV will handle everything

Factor	Buy on your own	Invest via crowdfunding
Keep up to date with growing number of landlord-related regulations	Landlords must comply or they risk huge fines	The SPV will handle everything
Spend valuable time dealing with tenant problems	Can be time consuming and stressful	The SPV will handle everything
Use available capital over a larger number of properties to spread risk	You can leverage your available funds by taking out mortgages but it leaves you vulnerable to interest rate changes and the small print in your mortgage deed should property values fall	Crowdfunding provides an ideal way for you to spread your risk over a large number of properties and with no risk of repossession
Vulnerable to interest rate rises	Yes	No
Void periods	Yes, you are vulnerable to void periods and non-payment of rent and you would still need to pay mortgage payments each month	Yes, there can be void periods but even if there are you will not need to make any interest payments as there is no debt (usually) on the property
Tenant problems	You or your agent will need to deal with tenant issues. Can be time consuming and emotionally draining	The SPV will deal with all problems

Chapter 13

All about peer-to-peer secured lending

Equity investments are not the only way to access property investing.

Peer-to-peer platforms have made lending, once the sole preserve of financial institutions and high net worth investors, available for retail investors to benefit from.

Although a relatively new concept, it is proving just as popular as equity crowdfunding as investors can benefit from fixed interest rates and fixed investment terms – often of just a few months.

Debt investments are frequently perceived as riskier than equity investments as there is no actual ownership of the asset. However, in reality, the opposite is true and, in the event of a default by the borrower, those who have the benefit of a legal charge will have the first call on monies from a sale – in exactly the same way as a mortgagor does.

How does it work?

Although there are a couple of peer-to-peer platforms that offer investment terms of several years – essentially providing mortgages – most peer-to-peer secured lending is focused on providing bridging loans and/or development finance (which pay higher returns to investors than mortgage type lending) and the investments are typically between six and 18 months in length.

By acting as an intermediary between borrowers and investors, thus cutting out the traditional institutional lenders, peer-to-peer secured lending enables retail investors to earn high rates of interest – often 710% p.a. – whilst giving them the security of having their investment protected by the underlying value of the borrower's property.

If the borrower defaults on the loan, the holder of the legal charge – a trustee acting on behalf of all investors – can take possession of the property and take steps to recover investors' money plus any interest owed.

Bridging finance, despite the high interest rates payable, appeals to borrowers for whom standard bank finance is either unsuitable, or unavailable. These borrowers are prepared to pay higher rates in order access funds quickly, often in order to secure a profitable deal, and therein lies the profit for the lender.

Who uses bridging loans?

Typical borrowers are investors buying at auction, property developers who are seeking to refurbish and 'flip' a property, or businesses who have short-term liquidity problems. For example, businesses often need short-term funding in order to raise capital, settle tax liabilities, deal with emergencies, meet business obligations, or to purchase necessary items for the company's use.

For property investors, landlords, developers, buyers and house builders, fast access to funding can mean the difference between securing a purchase, or losing it to competition.

Regular lenders can take months to complete a loan application, but a bridging loan can be acquired within a few days.

A property investor can therefore take advantage of opportunities as they arise, for example, to buy a property at discounted price. They are also useful in emergency situations, for example, should something occur within a property that must be fixed immediately.

These are a selection of typical bridging loan scenarios:

Example 1

Overview
The borrowers required additional funds to help launch their new business venture, and utilised a second home that they had in Derbyshire.

Client: Mr & Mrs C.
Purpose of loan: Raising funds for a new business venture
Amount: £330,000 gross
Period of Loan: 6 months
Defined Exit: Sale of the security
Security: A first charge against a second home in Derbyshire. Value of security was £850,000
LTV: 39%

Example 2

Overview
The borrowers required funds to help complete the purchase of an investment property. Funds were required to also consolidate a £75,000 business debt.

Client: Mr & Mrs Q.
Purpose of loan: Raising funds for a property purchase and business debt
Amount: £136,000 gross
Period of Loan: 12 months
Defined Exit: Sale of the security or refinance with Barclays
Security: A second charge against the borrower's property. Value of security was £2.4 million
LTV: 70%

Example 3

Overview
The borrowers required funds to help complete the purchase of an investment property in Florida. Funds were required within 10 days.

Client: Mr & Mrs S.
Purpose of loan: Raising funds to complete the purchase of an investment property in Florida.
Amount: £284,000 gross
Period of Loan: 6 months
Defined Exit: Refinance with HSBC
Security: A second charge against the borrower's property. Value of security was £1.3 million
LTV: 65%

Overview: Business Loan
Client: Mr & Mrs J.C/Company Directors
Purpose of loan: Raising funds for business cash flow and development
Amount: £100,000 gross
Period of Loan: 9 months
Defined Exit: Sale of stock. Also had second option of selling the security.
Security: A second charge against a holiday home in Wales. Value of security was £325,000.
LTV: 56%

Development finance

Development finance is very similar to bridging finance, in that it is lent on a short-term basis at rates of around 1.5% a month. As the name indicates, the loan must be used for the specific purpose of developing property, either existing or new-build, and will be secured against the land/property.

Small and medium sized developers have struggled in recent years to acquire bank finance and peer-to-peer lending platforms have provided them with a new source of funding. This has the dual benefit of providing developers with funds to build much needed housing and giving access for retail investors to very attractive returns – as high as 12% p.a.

Development finance is often perceived as riskier, because the value of the underlying security can fluctuate significantly during the build period (for example if an existing building is being demolished) and because unforeseen things can go wrong. It is, therefore, vital you carefully consider the feasibility of the project as well as the security aspect, before you invest as you may be reliant on the sale of the properties to return your capital and pay your return.

Gratrix Park

An executive development of 15 houses and four apartments in Sale, Greater Manchester.

Amount raised: £1,200,000
Interest rate paid: 10–12% depending on the sum invested
Security: first legal charge
Investment period: 11 months

Bollin Heights

The conversion of a 13,500 sq foot office building in Wilmslow town centre to apartments.

Amount raised: £3,500,000
Interest rate paid: 10–12% depending on sum invested
Security: first legal charge
Investment period: 8 months

Pros and cons of peer-to-peer secured lending

Let's take a look at the relative pros and cons:

Pros

Firstly, the potential returns are excellent – much higher than you can achieve with just about anything else including dividend yields.

The returns are fixed, and do not fluctuate like returns from equity investments or the stock market. You therefore know what to expect, provided the borrower does not default.

Lenders are not charged any fees so the amount stated is the net amount you receive.

Platforms no longer have to deduct tax at source, so you will be paid gross and account for your own tax.

The investment terms are short – typically under 12 months – so your money will only be tied up for a short period.

Legal charge holders will be paid out as a priority before any owners/equity shareholders.

It is FCA regulated which means platforms have to offer a high level of transparency and are legally obliged to be upfront about all risks involved in investing this way. They must also have contingency plans in place in case something goes wrong, such as a significant financial buffer should the platform itself suffer financial difficulties.

With the launch of the IFISA (Innovative Finance ISA) in April 2016, you can now hold peer-to-peer loans within an ISA, meaning that your returns are tax free. You can invest, at present, up to £15,240 per tax year into an ISA, whether in cash, peer-to-peer loans, or stocks and shares, or a combination of the three. However, at the time of writing the FCA and HMRC have a long list of firms waiting to be authorised to offer these ISAs and are progressing at a painfully slow rate.

Cons

Whilst regulated by the FCA, peer-to-peer lending is not covered by the Financial Services Compensation Scheme (FSCS). As such, losses are not underwritten by the government in the way that they would be if you'd put your money in a savings account with a bank. Your investment should, however, be protected by the value of the property.

Once you have made a peer-to-peer loan you are likely to be tied in until the borrower has repaid. There may be some chance the platform can find you a buyer but there is no guarantee. If you think you may need the money back before the expiry of the term then it is probably not wise to invest.

Though the loan periods are short, you may have to wait for the loan to complete before you start earning interest. The lag is not usually more than a few days or weeks, but until a loan is actively engaged, you will not be earning interest on your invested sum.

One alternative is to lend money to the finance company and get a fixed return for a fixed period – say 2 years. The rate will be less but your interest will be continuous so you are likely to end up with approximately the same return, but without having to select individual loans to invest in.

If the borrower does not repay on time you will need to wait until they have repaid – although you should continue to earn interest in the meantime.

If the borrower defaults, the property will have to be repossessed in order to sell it and pay back lenders. If that is the case, there are likely to be delays of several months at least. Further, there is a risk that the property will not achieve a sale price great enough for lenders to be repaid all their capital and/or the interest owed. Bear in mind that while you will receive a fixed rate of interest that may well be higher than average dividends, you will not benefit from any upside in capital growth.

Chapter summary

- Why debt-based investments are attractive for many investors.
- How the short-term (aka bridging) finance industry works.
- How debt-based investments are secured.
- Why development finance provides the best returns but carries the biggest risk.
- How to mitigate risk.
- An assessment of the pros and cons of secured lending
- Debt investments general provide higher income but no capital growth

Chapter 14

Commonly asked questions about property crowdfunding

How safe is my money?
There is no government safety net such as the FSCS. The value of your security lies in the value of the property you are buying or loaning money against. If that property has to be sold for less than the purchase price/amount lent, you would lose some or all of your capital.

Will I know the identity of the borrower when I make a peer-to-peer loan?
Loans made are known as micro-loans which are facilitated by the platform and pooled to form the whole amount of the loan. You will, with most platforms, receive full details of the property security and the terms of the loan. Whilst the platform will conduct due diligence on the borrower and their credit rating, the name of the borrower will not usually be disclosed to investors.

What is the liquidity?
The liquidity of each investment will vary. With equity investments, you may be able to sell your shares before the actual property has been sold, but the secondary market is restricted. There is no guarantee you will be able to do so and may have to wait as you would with an individual house sale for a buyer who is willing and able to buy at the desired price. In respect of loans there is usually a defined exit and set

loan redemption date, so you know what date to expect your money back – unless the borrower defaults.

Why are bridging loan rates so much higher than the banks?

Simply because the bridging industry charges higher rates to those people looking for short-term finance and for whom traditional bank loans are not suitable. This may be because the banks do not offer short-term secured loans or they would take too long to arrange, in which case the opportunity for the property owner will have passed.

Is there a risk of fraud?

It's possible and you should be aware that it could have very serious consequences if someone perpetrates a successful fraud. In order to mitigate this risk, every regulated platform should undertake thorough and proper checks on all borrowers and their solicitors.

Are returns guaranteed?

In short, no. Never. All investment carries a risk – even leaving your money in a bank account is not completely risk free. No company should ever tell you something is risk free. It must present the potential rewards and the potential risks clearly and fairly. It should explain how those risks are mitigated (e.g. how the investment is secured) but it is always possible there will be unforeseen problems. It is up to you to assess the risks and decide whether you are willing to accept them in exchange for the potential reward.

What can go wrong?

Essentially all the same things that can go wrong with a normal property investment – including the fact the property may not rent for some reason or it may have to be sold for less than you paid for it. Or in the case of a loan, the borrower may default and the property cannot be sold for more than the value of the loan. You also have the additional risks associated with loans of potential fraud perpetrated by the borrower.

How are investments protected?

In the case of equity investments, by ownership of the property via a shareholding in the SPV that purchases. In the case of a debt-based investment, by a legal charge over the borrower's land or property.

What happens if the platform gets into financial difficulty?

All investments, whether equity or peer-to-peer, should be ringfenced and protected by ownership of shares or legal charges. The platform itself should not (unless it has the permissions to do so) ever hold client funds. All FCA regulated platforms should have a 'living will' or succession plan in place so that should the crowdfunding company go into administration a suitable third party will take over the administration/liquidation of all investments and return capital to investors. Check what procedures a platform has in place before investing.

Can you invest in joint names or through a company?

With most platforms, it is possible to invest in individual names, joint names, in the name of a limited company or a trust and you could also invest on behalf of your children provided the money earned genuinely goes into a bank account for their benefit. Investing in different names is a great way to make the most of tax-free allowances but you will always need to provide the appropriate anti-money laundering information.

How will money be recovered if the borrower defaults on a loan?

At the lender's election, the borrower can be given extra time to repay the loan (typically up to three months). This will usually incur penalty interest. A responsible lender will look to help the borrower repay – perhaps by refinancing with another company or selling a property at auction. If the borrower has still not repaid at the end of any agreed extension period, the lender can apply for a court order for possession of the property. This is much easier to do if the loan is not secured against the borrower's primary residence. There can also be problems if your investment is secured by a second charge and the first charge holder decides to be obstructive.

When people make a peer-to-peer-loan, why is the legal charge not in the name of all lenders?

A legal charge at Companies House can only be held in a maximum of four names. Therefore, when more lenders are involved, the charge needs to be held by a trustee on behalf of all lenders. With actual property purchases, some companies also hold the shares as trustee on behalf of each investor. Whilst not strictly necessary, it does facilitate the administrative process and make selling of shares easier.

And, specifically relating to debt-based Investments, you should ask the following questions...

How is my money secured?

Investors' money should be secured against the borrower's property by way of a legal charge in the same way as a bank would secure a mortgage loan. If it is a second charge, bear in mind that the party with the benefit of a first charge will have priority (i.e. be paid out before) over second charge holders. Therefore, when making a peer-to-peer loan with a second charge you should ensure that

a) second charge holders can enforce a sale in the event of the borrower defaulting;
b) the LTV stated is based upon the equity remaining after the first charge holder has been repaid;
c) you have allowed for dropping the sale price to obtain a quick sale. At The House Crowd, for example, we only invest in properties with loan to value of less than 75% of the current RICS value of the property. This is to provide our investors with a decent sized cushion in the event that the borrower defaults and the property has to be sold quickly at a discount or the market falls for some reason during the period of the loan.

What due diligence is done on each loan?

All security valuations should be acquired by independent, RICS qualified surveyors from reputable firms with the required level of indemnity insurance in place. The surveyors should provide an open market value and a fire sale value (which is the price they believe could be obtained should the property have to be sold within 90 days). Valuations should be cross-referenced with the purchase price and if there is a discrepancy then an explanation with appropriate verification should be provided.

What checks does the solicitor perform?
They should check the identity of the borrower and the bona fides of the borrower's own solicitor. The solicitor should review and approve all loan, mortgage, legal title and other documents to ensure all is in order.

What is the loan to value and what is it based upon?
Is it the open market value, or the fire sale value? Is the interest payable included in the LTV calculation?

What level of security do investors receive?
Usually a first or second charge. If a second charge, check the LTV is based on the remaining equity.

What happens if the borrower does not repay on time?
Does the charge holder have the ability to repossess the property quickly in the event of default? It is much harder to force a sale of someone's primary residence, so this should be classed as an additional risk.

When is the interest paid?
Is it monthly or upon loan redemption?

Chapter 15

Comparison: equity crowdfunding v peer-to-peer

As I write at the start of 2017, it is true to say that, despite it regularly featuring in the media, the majority of people are still not familiar with what crowdfunding is and most have not even heard about property crowdfunding.

The alternative finance platforms to date have really only been used by what marketing people call 'early adopters' and the industry probably has a couple of years to go (at least) before it is truly adopted as an acceptable way to invest by the general population.

For the next five or six years it is forecast to grow at a phenomenal rate as it starts to reach a broader audience. Between 2015 and 2016, equity crowdfunding raised a combined total of £216.25 million and peer-to-peer facilitated a combined lending of £2.6 billion.

In equity crowdfunding, across the seven leading platforms, an average amount of £18 million was raised per month. Just under 400 deals were funded, with 800,000 investments being made.

As a result of investor confidence, an array of large fundraisers, and the general state of the broader macroeconomic environment, the period October 2015 to December 2015 demonstrated a high growth trend. There was a drop-off during 2016, but two major events from the year, the FTSE three-year low in January 2016, and the fallout from the EU referendum result, demonstrated that crowdfunding has firmly established itself within the investor market. In peer-to-peer lending, across the eight major platforms, £197 million was lent per month during the same period. August 2016 saw lending shoot up by 20%, demonstrating the biggest month-on-month increase to date. Following this, September 2016 subsequently resulted in the strongest performing month in the history of the peer-to-peer model, with total lending of close to £234 million.

Clearly, both these sectors of the alternative finance industry are showing strong growth in popularity.

Equity crowdfunding and peer-to-peer secured lending find them-selves grouped together under the term 'property crowdfunding'. However, the two, as we have seen, are quite distinct: each with their own qualities. So how do each of the models compare as potential additions to your investment portfolio? And given the prudence in diversification, it may well be worth you considering both types of investment. This will also allow you to benefit from the tax breaks available from both types of investments.

Property crowdfunding as a vehicle to invest in property can involve both debt and equity investments and both structures have exploded in popularity since they began four or five years ago.

Although they are often lumped together under the banner of 'property crowdfunding' and although both involve raising finance from a crowd of people who pool their resources, most people don't appre-ciate that crowdfunding and peer-to-peer lending are in some ways distinctly different.

Here's a quick recap

Equity crowdfunding means you acquire shares in a company in exchange for your investment. You will be entitled to a share of rental and sale income by way of dividend.

If there is no profit to be shared out, you will not receive a dividend.

If the property purchased falls in value it is likely your shares will do likewise and you may lose money.

Should you wish to sell your shares you are free to do so at any point provided you can find a buyer. Any profit you make upon sale of your shares will usually be subject to CGT (after the annual allowance has been taken into account).

It is important to recognise that although most people believe ownership provides them with more security, when an asset such as a house is sold, any loans taken out against that property are paid out before shareholders receive their dividend. The creditors therefore are in many ways in a stronger position than the actual property owner/shareholders.

Many people prefer equity crowdfunding because it gives them a sense of ownership – a real share in a property and a sense of something solid – and because they receive both the benefits of a profit from rental income and in any capital growth of the property.

Equity investments such as these where risk and reward are shared are normally regarded as Sharia compliant and suitable for Muslim investors – though that is a personal decision for each investor.

Alternatively, debt-based property crowdfunding or, to give it its commonly used name, peer-to-peer secured lending, tends to involve shorter investment periods of, typically, six to 12 months. Borrowers are people for whom normal bank finance is not suitable or not available and they are prepared to pay a high rate of interest for a short period. Typically, they are property developers looking to refurbish and flip a property or a business owner who needs cash on a short-term basis. They pay a premium for these short-term loans (aka bridging loans) which means the lenders can expect excellent rates of returns – typically 6–9% p.a.

Your money is secured against the borrower's property by the registration of a legal charge in the same way a bank secures a mortgage loan.

As noted above, lenders get priority over shareholders in terms of being paid out when the property is sold, which can make it a very secure investment provided you only invest in properties up to a modest loan to value in case the borrower defaults and the property has to be sold.

For example, at The House Crowd, we only invest in properties where the money lent is less than 75% of the RICS valuation of a property. That way there is a decent cushion should the property have to be sold quickly at a discount in order to repay lenders.

You do not receive any equity in the property and thus will not benefit from any capital growth but you will have the benefit of knowing what return you will receive and how long your money is likely to be tied up.

The bridging finance industry has been around for decades but crowdfunding companies now enable small investors to get involved in this lucrative market by making loans of just a few hundred pounds.

Peer-to-peer lending is now available under the Innovative Finance ISA wrapper, making your returns tax free.

Peer-to-peer lending is not Sharia compliant as interest is paid to investors.

Here's a simple chart so you can compare the main factors side by side:

Property crowdfunding V Peer-to-peer secured lending	
How do they work?	
A crowd of people pooling resources to buy a property. Profit and losses are shared proportionately.	Cutting out the banks, property developers/investors borrow directly from a crowd of individuals with each person contributing part of the loan required. By doing so borrowers can raise money more easily and lenders may receive a better return on their money.
Type of investment	
Crowdfunding is an equity investment. You own shares in a company that buys the property.	As a lender you are lending directly to the borrower and your money is secured by way of a registered legal charge against a property. The investment is classed as a debt.
Returns	
You receive a share of all profits generated including a pro rata share of both rental income and any capital growth. You are paid by way of dividends or by redeeming or selling your shares. If the property has to be sold at a loss you will lose a portion of your money. If the property does not achieve its forecast rental income or if maintenance costs are higher than forecast, you will receive less than expected.	You are entitled to receive a set amount of interest regardless of whether the borrower makes any profit. The returns offered will be decided by the level of security and the length of the loan period. Typically, the returns will be 6–10% p.a. You will not be entitled to any share of profit or capital growth. Nor will you be responsible for any losses.

Security	
You will be a part owner (shareholder) in the company that owns the property. Your rights are protected by the company's Articles.	Loans are secured by way of a registered legal charge against the property. That means that if the loan is not repaid with the agreed interest the lenders can force the sale of the property and recover what they are owed the same way a bank can do if a borrower does not repay their mortgage.
Liquidity	
Both property and shares in unlisted companies are illiquid assets and both may be hard to sell. You may not be able to find a buyer for your shares and may have to wait until the property is sold.	Loans are for a fixed period: typically, 6–12 months. You will receive your capital and money back at the end of the term, unless the borrower defaults. A default may lead to possession proceedings and can take months to resolve.
Payment: order of priority	
Shareholders are paid out after any secured creditors have been paid.	Lenders are paid as the first order of priority. It is the highest level of security. However, if P2P lenders have a second charge, the first charge holder (e.g. a bank) will be paid out first in the order of priority. There is a risk that first charge holders may obstruct a possession and sale.
Regulated?	
Equity crowdfunding investments are regulated by the FCA.	P2P loans are regulated by the FCA.

As mentioned in earlier chapters, it is sensible to diversify and spread your risk. It is likely, therefore, to make sense if you spread your investments over both equity- and debt-based investments and benefit from the tax breaks afforded to both.

Chapter 16

What returns can you expect?

With peer-to-peer loans the answer is simple: whatever the stated rate is. Provided the borrower does not default, that is what you will receive. With longer-term secured lending it's likely to be 2–4%, with bridging loans 6–9% and with development finance 8–12%.

As far as equity investments go, you will share proportionately in the profits from rental income and any capital growth (which is speculative but can provide a very large uplift to overall returns). So the short answer is that it depends. There are a range of factors that can influence the return on investment to be gained from a property.

Firstly, there is the matter of the property itself. Its location, and what type of property it is, are both crucial factors that will affect your return. As we have explored in earlier, a substantial amount of work and analysis is required in order to achieve the best possible returns.

It has over the last decade been a general rule that the further north you go in England, the higher the yields but the lesser the potential for capital growth. However, Manchester, and its surrounding towns, seems to have hit a sweet spot where yields are high and, given a number of macroeconomic factors – the re-birth of Salford, Media City, its popularity with students and graduates and massive investment in regeneration programmes and its ability to attract major companies – the potential for capital growth is thought by many to be the strongest in the country.

Here is a summary of some of the top yielding areas in 2016 to give you an idea of what is achievable (and what you should expect from a crowdfunding platform):

Top spot goes to Manchester, with an average yield of 6.8%. As people flee the unaffordability of London, Manchester is often their first choice city. The same applies to investors who have been snapping up properties in the UK's favourite city ... okay, I may be a little biased here (being Manchester born and bred), but the fact remains that Manchester, according to almost every recent survey, is the most profitable place to rent out a property in the UK.

Coventry and Luton with average yields of 5.8% should be next on any landlord's target list, though Luton probably represents a stronger market for capital appreciation.

Some areas of outer London are (surprisingly) still able to deliver yields of around 5.7% but they are getting harder to achieve all the time.

Blackburn/Oldham and certain other areas around Manchester are also achieving yields of around 5.7%.

Forecasts for capital growth are as we know speculative and based on a whole load of subjective assumptions. There is evidence that shows property prices have doubled on average every 10 years throughout the last 60 odd years but there is no guarantee as to what they will do over the next 10 years. With 20 years' experience of tracking what property experts forecast the only thing I have learned is they are wrong a lot more often than they are right. After all, there are so many things they cannot possibly predict. But, for what it's worth, this is how property values may increase over the next five years, according to Savills (probably the most reliable source).

East England – 19%
South East – 17%
South West – 14%
Midlands – 13.5%
North West – 12%
London – 11%
Wales – 10%
Yorkshire – 10%
North East – 9%
Scotland – 9%

When calculating the returns you can expect, you must establish the difference between gross yield of a property (which is the annual rent received divided by the cost of the property) and the net return to you.

You will need to take into account the fees charged by the platform for its work in raising the funds, managing the asset, handling the company secretarial work and selling the property. This is likely to reduce the gross yield by several per cent.

This is a typical equity-based deal we offer at The House Crowd:

Stanhope Street

Like many of the equity deals we offer, this is a property that is let on a commercial basis to a large corporation on a five-year lease and fixed rental. The tenant is also responsible for routine maintenance of up to £5,000 a year. I believe this type of assured rental deal takes a lot of the uncertainty out of buy-to-let. The properties produce a gross yield of around 9.5% and the annual net return to investors is usually

5.6%. These properties are valued as commercial premises as they have been converted into houses in multiple occupation (HMOs) and therefore, the valuations are based on the rent they produce, and they will normally be valued significantly higher than a similar single family dwelling on the same street. It does mean that if you want to make a profit on sale you will probably need to sell to an investor rather than a home owner which may prove more difficult

Chapter 17

Taxation

You should always take your own tax advice from a qualified accountant (and I am not one). The following is, therefore, accurate as far as I am aware but is for general information purposes only.

Equity investments in property owning SPVs: SPVs are limited companies incorporated in the United Kingdom and as such they are subject to corporation tax, currently at the rate of 20%, on their net rental income and they will also pay corporation tax at the same rate on any capital gains arising on a subsequent sale of the property.

Following the sale of the property and the final distribution to shareholders, whilst the shareholders will not be liable to capital gains tax on the actual sale of the property as this will already have been paid by the SPV itself, they may if they are UK resident be liable to capital gains tax on the excess of the final distribution over the original cost of their shares at the rate of 10% for basic rate taxpayers or 20% for higher rate taxpayers. If they have no other capital gains in the year of disposal they will also have available their annual Capital Gains Tax exemption of £11,100 to offset against the gain.

Until such time as a sale of the property takes place annual dividends are paid out of the SPV's profits after taxation.

Each shareholder is entitled to an annual tax free dividend allowance of £5,000 so no tax is payable on this amount of dividends received in each tax year.

Dividends received within this allowance will still count towards a shareholder's income when calculating their basic or higher rate tax bands. For dividends received in excess of this amount in any tax year the rates of tax payable are: 7.5% on income within the basic rate tax band of £1 to £32,000; 32.5% on income within the higher rate band of £32,001 to £150,000; and 38.1% on income in the additional rate band in excess of £150,000.

For UK corporate shareholders the dividends would be received as franked investment income and excluded from their taxable profit for corporation tax purposes because the income has already suffered corporation tax.

As far as peer-to-peer loans are concerned, gross interest received needs to be declared and will be charged at the rate applicable to the individual. In 2015 the chancellor stated that no tax will be deducted on the first £1,000 of interest earned every year on savings from April 2016. So you may earn up to £1,000 in interest tax free.

So, by combining allowances for equity and debt based investments you can earn £6,000 per year tax free.

Additionally, with the launch of the IFISA (Innovative Finance ISA) in April 2016, you can now also hold peer-to-peer loans (but not currently equity crowdfunding investments) within an ISA, meaning that your returns are tax free. You can invest, at present, up to £15,240 per tax year into an ISA, whether in cash, peer-to-peer loans, or stocks and shares, or a combination of the three.

Chapter summary

There are tax free allowances for both dividend income and interest and it makes sense to take advantage of both of them by diversifying.

Chapter 18

How to decide whether crowdfunding is right for you

The first question to ask yourself is how crowdfunding sits within your personal circumstances. Are you an experienced investor? What is it you want to achieve through your investments?

Crowdfunding has opened up the world of property investment to a much wider range of investors. People who, previously, would have struggled to get started in this potentially lucrative form of investment, now have the opportunity to do so through this medium.

Whilst there are, of course, pros and cons, property crowdfunding is an easier, safer and simpler way to grow your money.

If you are already a professional property investor with ready access to bank funding, then crowdfunding is less likely to appeal to you. You will know how to successfully invest on your own, reap good profits, and keep more of them.

When you invest in a crowdfunding platform, you are leveraging the skills of other professionals in order to make a financial return. If you are just starting out, as a novice investor without the time and access to funding, then crowdfunding might offer you an attractive solution.

If you don't have funds to put down a large enough deposit, or you are not yet able to get a mortgage, then crowdfunding offers you the opportunity to invest in property without a massive financial outlay. It may act as an excellent introduction to property investment, allowing you to grow your knowledge and understanding of the market, whilst raising the necessary funds to either go it alone, or reap returns on an asset class that you would otherwise struggle to access.

As well as reducing the amount of time and money traditionally required to invest in property, there is another benefit to crowdfunded property investment. Some argue that, by investing with a company who sources, purchases and manages the property also mitigates investor risk. Professionals, who are experienced and knowledgeable, will be able to make wise, informed decisions of which a novice may not have full understanding. Furthermore, some people feel that investing with a crowd of other investors leaves them less exposed.

On the other hand, others argue that, simply because several people are investing in something, it doesn't necessarily mitigate all the risks, many of which are the same as investing in property on one's own. Arguably, this comes down to your personal views, and it is important to weigh up the pros and cons to make the right decision.

With property crowdfunding, you are usually bound by a stipulated investment term or reliant on a majority shareholder vote in order to sell the property. Although there is the possibility you can sell your shares and the platform may help you to do so, there is no guarantee a buyer can be found. If, therefore, you like to be in control of your investments, and it is important for you to be able to liquidate them when you choose, then property crowdfunding may not be the right vehicle for you (though there is never any guarantee you will be able to sell a property you own outright – at least not for your desired price).

As we have discussed in previous chapters, crowdfunding frees you of the concerns of managing tenants, maintaining the property, and other financial, legal and practical aspects of the investment process. But if you wish to be able to personally control these aspects yourself, then investing in property in the traditional manner may be a more suitable course.

The final thing to consider is your risk tolerance. Whilst many would argue that there is a decreased risk of investment loss with property crowdfunding, others would disagree. The risks have been outlined in this book, but if you need further clarification, then consulting a professional adviser may be the right course of action for you, although, be warned: as an IFA's professional indemnity insurance will not cover them advising on unregulated investments, it is highly unlikely they will see fit to recommend them.

Chapter 19

Key factors to consider when choosing a property crowdfunding platform

If you have decided you want to dip your toe in the water and give crowdfunding a try, there are now a large number of platforms to choose from.

My company, The House Crowd, was the first equity-based property crowdfunding platform to launch, but others such as Property Moose and Crowdlords followed in 2013, and there are a plethora of others that have started up more recently following very similar business models.

If you have more of a speculative mentality, like the idea of greater liquidity and being able to trade shares then Property Partner offers you the ability to do that.

As far as peer-to-leer lending goes you can choose between The House Crowd (the only platform to offer both types of investment), Lend Invest, Landbay, Crowd Property and various others.

These are some of the key factors to consider when selecting a platform.

Returns

The first factor is the most obvious: What are the returns on offer? The returns you will receive are based on how well the property performs, so a useful guide is to see where the properties are based and how well rental yields perform in that area. Then ask yourself: 'Do the yields being offered by the platform beat the averages for that area?' If not, then you should question what benefit the platform is providing and whether it is worthwhile investing with them. I must admit, I see many investments offered on platforms which are offering well-below-average yields for the area.

Check how far the promised returns take into account platform fees, and make sure you are clear on the actual return on investment after all other costs have been deducted.

Use the material in this book to assess for yourself whether the property on offer is well chosen and likely to beat average returns. If not, look elsewhere.

Yield v capital growth

People invest for different reasons and many are happy to only achieve a low yield as they are confident in the prospects for capital growth.

However, profits from capital growth are speculative and if you want to minimise your risk, I believe you should invest in those properties which produce a healthy cash flow. If the property is putting money in your pocket every year, then you will not be under pressure to sell and can wait for the optimum time to liquidate and benefit from the capital appreciation.

The biggest risk associated with investing in cash flow positive properties is damage and/or non-payment of rent. This needs to be factored in as it will happen at some point and yields will be affected.

One major benefit of crowdfunding is that if you diversify and have money spread over, say, ten properties, the losses caused by one bad tenant are easier to bear than if you had all your money in that one property. You can also spread your investment over speculative capital growth properties and income producing properties.

Security and risk

The target demographic for most property crowdfunding companies tends to be people who are unhappy with conventional savings accounts and disgruntled landlords. And this target group tends to be risk averse. Ask: how will your investment be protected? If it goes wrong, how much equity is there to enable you to recover your money?

> Buy-to-let with no mortgage = lower risk/decent return.
> Purchase with a mortgage = higher risk/potentially higher returns
> Development or bridging finance = possibly higher risk/potentially much higher and shorter-term returns

It's all very well a platform offering a high return, for example, on a development finance deal, but what happens if the developer goes bust? You must check what security there is in place to help recover your capital if it all goes wrong. Unless there is sufficient equity in the property you may be at risk of losing some or all your money. Standard buy-to-lets are generally more secure as the property already exists and there are fewer things that can go badly wrong. But, in a longer-term buy-to-let investment, you should make sure you are protected either by ownership of the property via your shareholding in an SPV or a charge registered at the Land Registry.

What happens if your dividend is not paid? This could be a risk if there are third party landlords/developers involved where they simply do not pay the dividends that are due. If that happens, how are you protected? For example, is there a default mechanism in the SPV's articles allowing shareholders to force a sale if the returns due are not paid?

Is the investment being offered by a company associated with the platform itself or an unrelated third party?

The fourth key factor is to ask yourself: do the platforms provide their own properties and third party offerings, or just their own properties? If it is an investment being offered by an SPV associated with the platform itself then it should tell you that the platform is taking responsibility for the investments it promotes and delivering the returns.

Be wary of platforms who may focus on raising funds for anyone who wants to list their investment on the site (and earn money from doing so). Platforms with integrity, which care about long-term reputation, will conduct thorough due diligence on the investment and the people behind it before allowing them to promote any property on their platform. So, if the investment is being offered by an unconnected third party (e.g. a private landlord or property developer), then you should ask what due diligence has been conducted on that third party, consider what their track record is and look at what additional safeguards are in place.

Track record of success and transparency

The next essential is finding out who are the people running the platform? After all, it will be their judgement about the right investment properties to buy. Look for people who have a proven track record in property investment. Look for people who are experienced investors themselves with a portfolio of their own properties.

As property crowdfunding becomes increasingly popular, there have already emerged platforms run by people inexperienced in property who are just looking to jump on what they perceive as a lucrative bandwagon.

As anyone who has bought their own buy-to-let property knows: finding good deals is hard, and managing a property portfolio even harder. Even if you use letting agents it is burdensome and things go wrong frequently. We employ two people just to manage the letting agents who manage the actual properties. You need to be confident that the people protecting your investment have the knowledge and ability to make the right decisions.

Check how long the crowdfunding company has been trading. Can they show a history of successful investments and a track record of paying out dividends on time? With regard to transparency, do they make you aware of the potential pitfalls (as they are obliged to do) as well as the benefits to the investment?

Exit

The sixth factor to consider is how easy is it for you to get your money back when you want it.

One drawback of property crowdfunding is that as an investor you will have little control over when the property is sold. If you think you might need your money back at short notice, it is probably not the right investment for you.

With most platforms you will be making an investment in shares which improves liquidity to some degree but it still may take a while to sell those shares and there is no guarantee you will be able to do so.

As we have detailed in this book, debt-based investments can afford you greater liquidity with terms of under 12 months and defined exits but even then there are risks that you won't get your money back on time.

Check the small print to see if the companies will assist you in finding a buyer for your shares or loan parts. It's unlikely there will be any guarantees to do so but secondary markets are beginning to emerge.

Customer service

The final key factor in finding the right property crowdfunding platform for you is that hardy perennial: customer service. There is nothing more frustrating than working with a company that does not look after you once it has taken your money.

There is no way to know this definitively, but test them to see how quickly they respond to enquiries and deal with complaints. Are they easy to contact? Are they helpful and informative in dealing with you or do they come across as pushy sales people? Are they clear about the risks and their regulatory obligations? Are there testimonials and case studies on their website? Search online for reviews and find out how others have found their service; for example, Trust Pilot carry independent reviews and ratings of a number of the most established crowdfunding platforms.

Chapter 20

Using your pension to invest via crowdfunding

A pension is simply a way in which you can save money in a tax efficient wrapper provided you adhere to certain rules.

There are two main options when it comes to your pension fund. Firstly, you can invest directly in property or you may be able to borrow money from your pension fund and use it to invest in property. Whether you are able to do so will depend upon your age, the size of your pension fund, the type of pension you have and the type of property you want to invest in.

There are a few flexible pensions – SIPPS and SASS – that allow investment in certain types of property without you having to withdraw funds and incur the resulting tax liability. An independent financial adviser (IFA) will be able to advise you, based on your personal circumstances and financial goals on which would allow you to make property investments. But the opportunities to do so are extremely limited.

In April 2015 George Osbourne, the then Chancellor, introduced the 'pension freedom' reforms. These have given people greater power over how they spend, save or invest their pension pot.

Major changes involved removing the need to buy an annuity and giving access to invest-and-drawdown schemes which were previously restricted to those with larger pensions. But the most widely publicised change is that people can now dip in and withdraw up to 25% of their pension pot tax free. The rest, however, will be subject to tax as though it was income.

So since April 2015, over-55s have been able to cash in all of their pension, and quite a few took the opportunity to invest at least part of their funds into property.

As we have seen, the benefits of doing so, even if you had enough to pay a large deposit or buy outright, have diminished considerably in the last year or so and the future is now not looking so rosy. Coupled with the time-consuming hassles attached to being a landlord, which is not appealing to most people in their so-called retirement years, it may well be that crowdfunding is the best way forward for those seeking to switch all or part of their pensions into property.

Everyone's circumstances are different and if possible you should get financial advice.

The government is offering everyone free sessions explaining about pension freedom, but these won't provide you with personalised advice. The advisers certainly will not advise on investment funds or how to effectively manage your money. You can turn to a financial adviser, who will charge an initial fee plus an ongoing annual fee if you want your investments reviewed and redistributed effectively on a regular basis.

The cost of financial help has fallen in the last couple of years but is still prohibitively expensive for many. If you can't afford advice or don't think it's worth the expense, then you will need to do your own homework.

Given that the returns from property crowdfunding can be significantly higher, it may well be worth you considering taking some of your pension money and diversifying into either equity crowdfunding or peer-to-peer lending. As we saw in the taxation chapter, you can currently earn £5,000 worth of dividend income per year tax free and £1,000 worth of income from interest tax free, should you wish to make peer-to-peer loans.

Further, with the arrival of the Innovative Finance ISA, each person could invest £15,240 per year in peer-to-peer loans and the income would be tax free.

One important final point to realise is that once you purchase an annuity you will receive the applicable rate for the rest of your life but when you pass away the insurance company keeps the capital. If you were to purchase a house or make peer-to-peer loans, your heirs would be entitled to inherit the property of the capital. If you are concerned about your heirs, this is a vital point to consider.

For illustrative purposes only, here's a comparison of how your returns might compare over 20 years if you have a £100,000 pension pot.

Assumptions

1) Purchase an annuity for £100,000.
2) Withdraw £25,000 tax free and invest in P2P loans and buy an annuity with £75,000.
3) Withdraw all £100,000, pay tax on £75,000 and invest it all in P2P loans.

Cumulative Income and Capital

Legend:
- Leave £100,000 in pension with an annuity of £4,000 pa
- Draw down £25,000 (tax free) and invest in P2P loans @ 8% pa
- Draw down £100,000 and invest in P2P loans at 8%
- Draw down £100,000 and invest in B2L @ 5.5% and 4% Cap Growth

End Value
£80,000
£125,000
£207,380
£263,223

X-axis: Yr 1, Yr 2, Yr 3, Yr 4, Yr 5, Yr 6, Yr 7, Yr 8, Yr 9, Yr 10, Yr 11, Yr 12, Yr 13, Yr 14, Yr 15, Yr 16, Yr 17, Yr 18, Yr 19, Yr 20

Y-axis: £0, £50,000, £100,000, £150,000, £200,000, £250,000, £300,000, £350,000, £400,000

Chapter 21

Crowdfunding your own property deals

And, finally, what about the other side of the coin... what if you as a property developer, a house flipper, landlord or other property entrepreneur want to raise money for your own projects via a crowdfunding platform.

Banks and traditional mortgage lenders always want to know a borrower's personal credit history and income, and usually limit the amount of finance they will allow a borrower to have at any one time. Many small developers face similar problems when it comes to funding their developments – not least of which are the harsh penalties for default and such people may not want or may not be able to get finance from banks.

Whilst many small developers and property wheeler dealers have private investors willing to back their projects, that money is always finite and will inevitably run out after a while. Property crowdfunding platforms enable such entrepreneurs to tap into a much larger investor network and gives them access to virtually unlimited amounts of cash... There aren't many people with £1,000,000 to invest in a property deal but there are millions with £10,000 available who are looking for an attractive return.

But while crowdfunding money is plentiful and quick, it's not likely to be cheap. Investors are willing to be consider deals that might not fit a bank's criteria but they are looking for attractive returns in exchange for what is perceived as a moderately high risk investment. There is a considerable amount of marketing and administration required by the platform who also need to make a margin. You are likely, therefore, to be either agreeing to a substantial slice of equity or a double digit fixed rate return.

If you are an investor or developer then clearly the factors you will need to consider are the comparative cost of finance, speed of raising money and flexibility of the lender/ investor and how much you will make from the deal.

The good crowdfunding platforms – ones with a large and trusting database of clients – will want to see that you have a proven track record and will undertake appropriate due diligence on your opportunity before promoting it.

Each crowdfunding site operates in slightly different ways and accepts different sorts of deals. Lend Invest or Crowd Property for example will make secured loans against property, Crowd Lords offer landlords and developers the ability to raise money on a shared equity basis. And The House Crowd offers equity deals, secured loans and development finance.

Secured loans offered on crowdfunding platforms tend to be short term and you are likely to be paying a significantly higher rate than a typical buy to let mortgage and usually around the same as standard bridging loan rates – 1%-1.5% a month plus fees.

There is no guarantee that you will be able to raise the money and it will obviously depend on how attractive the deal is for investors. If you are prepared to share the profits though, it can reduce the risks as you will not be obligated to make mortgage payments every month.

Crowdfunding works particularly well for 'house flippers' and other short term develop and sell projects as it means you simply share the profits out when the property is sold. Whereas longer term buy-to-let joint ventures will involve a considerable amount of administration to keep investors updated and pay out dividends on a regular basis. It involves a lot of trust, on the platform's behalf, in respect of the landlords and I know, from my perspective, I would only work with people I knew and trusted and where we could keep control over the money to ensure everyone was paid.

But if you can offer attractive deals and are prepared to share the wealth, you could have an endless source of JV finance and never need to apply for a mortgage again.

Here are my six top tips for a successful crowdfunding campaign:

1. Make sure you can provide evidence of a credible property background with a proven track record and a number of successful projects behind you. You are unlikely to get backing as a novice from the crowd and would be better off seeking money from those who know and trust you.

2. Choose your platform carefully. There are a plethora of new property crowdfunding platforms and many will not have sufficient databases to successfully funds deals. Choose one that has successfully funded a decent number of sizeable and similar projects to yours.

3. Be generous with the terms you are prepared to offer. There are many attractive deals available that people can choose to invest in. If you want a successful campaign – share the upside and be generous, especially if you are trying to build your reputation.

4. Always under promise and overdeliver. True of any business. And always allow a contingency for unforeseen problems, because there definitely will be some.

5. Prepare a strong investment case with lots of market information and comparables. You need to sell yourself and your project to convince them they should invest with you. Just because you believe it's a great deal doesn't mean it will be obvious to them why that is the case.

6. Take great photographs or provide quality CGIs. Yes, investment should be all about the numbers and pretty pictures really shouldn't matter, but they do. Trust me. It's not always possible to acquire good images and some of the best deals are for unattractive properties but do so wherever possible.

Chapter 22

FCA regulated Companies

These are some of the main reputable players in the alternative finance sector. These are not recommendations. Please do your own due diligence before investing via any platform.

Equity crowd-funding platforms	Specialisms	Website
The House Crowd	Northern Powerhouse specialists. Assured fixed rentals investments.	www.thehousecrowd.com
Property Moose	Traditional terraced and buy-to-let stock. Mainly in the North East.	www.propertymoose.co.uk
Property Partner	London and new-build apartments. Share trading platform gives higher level of liquidity.	www.propertypartner.co
Transcendent Real Estate	Equity investments in commercial property.	www.t-re.co.uk

Peer-to-peer platforms	Specialisms	Website
Crowd Property	Development finance. Typical rate payable – 8%	www.crowdproperty.com
The House Crowd	Secured bridging and development finance. Typical return: 8– 10%	www.thehousecrowd.com
Landbay	Buy-to-let mortgages. Typical return – 3.75%	www.landbay.co.uk
Lend Invest	Typical return 6–7%	www.lendinvest.com
Wellesley	Mortgages/secured lending. Typical return – 2.35%	www.wellesley.co.uk

Chapter 23

In conclusion

I hope this book has provided you with enough material for you to make an informed choice about whether you want to use crowdfunding platforms to invest in property and, if so, what to look out for to make sure you invest successfully.

I have tried to cover all the ground in an easy-to-read style and not make anything too complicated. However, if you think there are things I have missed or you think I could have explained something more clearly, please feel free to email me at info@thehousecrowd.com and I will respond to you as soon as possible.

Wishing you many excellent returns.

18153696R00060

Printed in Poland
by Amazon Fulfillment
Poland Sp. z o.o., Wrocław